THE COFFEE OF MEXICO

Origin & destiny

El Libro
CAFÉ DE MÉXICO
Origen y destino

PRESENTATION

The coffee of Mexico is served on tables in 45 countries around the world; its quality is recognized in all five continents.

Mexico occupies the ninth place in world production and exports two out of three beans of the coffee it produces. The annual value of the yield is estimated on 900 million dollars.

In addition, we are the second place in the planet in organic coffee production, and one of the main gourmet coffee producers.

More tan half a million producers cultivate coffee trees, most of them in indigenous areas, and the production and processing of the bean benefits more than three million families.

President Enrique Peña Nieto promotes a National Coffee Policy, under which the Secretary of Agriculture, Livestock, Rural Development, Fisheries and Food carries out the Program Procafé and Productive Impulse to Coffee.

The emphasis is on innovation, technological development and technical support of producers, primarily those located in areas of high poverty and marginalization, as a way to democratize productivity and improve their living standards and income.

The Government of the Republic has a program for the renovation and reforestation of coffee plantations, with the support of 400 certified and equipped technicians.

In technical and communal nurseries more than 30 million plants are produced annually, and we work in the renewal of shrubs in 75 thousand hectares, with a six- year goal of 250 thousand hectares.

Currently the National Center for Research, Innovation and Technological Development of Coffee is operating with a focus on the development of new technologies and varieties that will adapt to the new times of Mexican coffee production and make it more productive and profitable for domestic producers.

The aim is to restore, modernize, and make coffee production more profitable and productive, from the organization of producers, the integration of the production chain, and the establishment of synergies with all those involved.

Mexico participates in the International Coffee Organization, through SAGRAPA, and is currently the Vice President of the Committees for the Market Promotion and Development, and Projects, and is an active member of the Finance and Administration Committee.

The purpose of this book is to disseminate the achievements of Mexican coffee, strengthen its national and international presence, and show consumers the excellence of our country's aromatic.

It is an open and dynamic text, whose primary objective is to maintain its relevance so it will be constantly updated, with the help of the entire coffee community in an interactive effort, product of a permanent, democratic and participatory convention.

It is also a recognition to each of the participants in the various processes of the production chain, from planting and care in hilly regions, to its tasting and presence in the tables of Mexico and many other nations.

We hope that the reader will appreciate and enjoy this volume, and that it will contribute to value more and learn more about the coffee of Mexico, a product that transcends its consumption, for its part of the national history, economy and culture.

José Eduardo Calzada Rovirosa
Secretary of Agriculture, Livestock, Rural Development, Fisheries and Food.

BOARD

THE COFFEE OF MEXICO

INTRODUCTION

The origin of the coffee tree, precious bush where the gem that brings us the fruit of coffee blooms, is lost in the depth of time and the tropical forest in ancient Ethiopia.

Among the evergreen foliage of its resplendent leaves, clusters of ruby colored cherries appear, which follow snowy blooms affirmed by lavish rains and the solar brightness of this wide strip north and south of the Equator, which moves around the aqua-terrestrial globe between the astronomical lines of the signs of Cancer and Capricorn, in the $23° 27'$ parallel.

The fruit contains two bluish green almonds when it's damp, protected by a hard plastic shell, beige, called parchment that, in turn, is surrounded by mucilage. These components break away when the fruit is fermented, washed or naturally dried, or processed, so the pale seed, readily dehydrated, or the unwashed brown, is disposed to be roasted, grinded and generally prepared as the drink we know traditionally. However, technological development has allowed other forms of preparation, as is the case of decaffeinated extracts, capsules, known solubles and lyophilized ones. Furthermore, a varied array of gastronomic recipes is derived in jams liquors and food.

The wine of the intellect, whose attributes venture scientific hypotheses about its role in the evolution of the brain, comes from different plant varieties and their natural or human-induced hybrids. Each one has specific and common characteristics that are finally reflected in the aroma, flavor, acidity, body and other elements of a professional tasting that distinguishes differentiated or specialty coffees from standard ones. The most recognized commercial varieties are Arabica and Robusta.

Arabica coffee arrived to Mexico, it acclimated to our Mesoamerican geography and rooted in varied and fertile soils, especially in those of volcanic origin between the late 19th and early 20th century. From the islands of Martinique and Guadeloupe, in the Caribbean, it was cultivated markedly

in the Hacienda Guadalupe, in Córdoba, Veracruz, having passed through Cuba.

The green of its foliage, the white of its flowers, and the red of its fruits were also assimilated to the colors of our national flag.

More than two centuries of history, tradition and creole and mestizo culture on the fertile and generous nature accompany the coffee community that has been purified to form a large community made up of producers and farmworkers, processors and industrialists, traders and exporters, transporters, from "droves of mules" to trucks, ships and airplanes; also of providers of fertilizers, inputs, machinery, equipment and various professional and financial services.

The production value chain can be integrated both vertically as horizontally to incorporate new possibilities in the use of other products and by-products resulting from "bio-nano-technological" research.

In this book we intend to present the key elements of a whole universe associated with its fruit and the roasted bean used to prepare the most popular drink in the west, the second product of global economic exchange and from which over one hundred millions of human beings get their income and which twelve hundred million consumers enjoy.

Of unquestionable utility in the preservation of the balance of the ecosystem and the sustainability of the globe and a significant portion of the national territory, it is also a factor of political stability, social and cultural advancement.

A sustainable coffee production means:

- More production, productivity and income equitably distributed among its generators.
- More individual and collective welfare of producers,

workers and rural communities.
- More competitiveness and cooperation.
- More governance of markets.
- More environmental balance.
- More cafés, bars and places for the enjoyment and conviviality.

All with a warm mixture of Coffee for Peace, from Mexico to the world.

Coffee is a controversial topic, it generates debate and encourages dialectics, and it stimulates creative imagination. For some reason, revolutionary ideas of change have been gestated in its establishments since the time of Constantinople. The printed version of the book The Coffee of Mexico, with its digital adaptation, is just the beginning of a large and complex topic, with many constants and variables; so wide and deep that it makes up what is called the Science of Coffee.

From the map of the coffee genome, whose sequence has been outlined, to its applications in plantations –with or without sustainability criteria- as well as high technology processes, studies on taste, tolerance and neuronal stimuli in the consumer, occupy the tasks of research and higher education centers in different countries around the world.

In the case of Mexico there are several centers for agricultural research and education for the production of genetic material resistant to pests and diseases of the coffee tree. Packages of technical support, training and extension, promoted by the bodies that duly covered the gradual withdraw of the Mexican Coffee Institute, as well as their respective jobs, try to be articulated through the founding of the National Center for Research, Innovation and Technological Development of Coffee, in research, education, promotion and their link to the practice to transfer technology and innovate improving the productivity.

As for geopolitical economic, the United Nations (UN) and its related entities, such as the International Coffee Organization (ICO) deal with diplomacy between producing and consumer states. Meanwhile, within each country, there are different dependencies concurrent to the promotion programs of coffee production. The Secretariat of Agriculture, Livestock,

Rural Development, Fisheries and Food (SAGARPA) is responsible for coordinating the action of the Mexican state in its three levels of government and the initiatives of the private and social sectors.

This is an open and dynamic book that will continue to me made with the help of the entire coffee community in an interactive effort, product of a permanent democratic participatory convention that will integrate an encyclopedic dictionary.

The fate of Mexican coffee production will be determined by the community involved, recovering our cultural tradition and modernizing programs, policies and tools to exploit the potential brought by the consumption of a growing population, in our territory as well as migrants in the United States and Canada (NAFTA), accustomed by the proven feasibility and profitability that it has in the broad productive horizon of bio-diverse ecosystems of the tropical mountain.

Therefore, in addition to communal and technical nurseries, a seedbed of producers is being carried out with a focus on children of coffee areas under an experiential educational method. The rejuvenation of old plantations, damaged by rust, the generational replacement of the productive forces and the modernization of our strategies, along with creative financing formulations, market intelligence and risk management, will bring us closer to the recovery of the historical role that Mexico has performed in this important activity.

CONTENTS

Origin

HISTORY AND LEGEND

HISTORY AND LEGEND

Going back to the origin of coffee implies the assumption of a way of thinking. Concrete facts are mixed with legends or fantastic stories. Although the most basic document search puts Ethiopia as the birthplace of the shrub, there are people who to the question where does coffee come from would undoubtedly respond Arabia. There are reasons for this supposition. On the subject, the most ancient writings refer that the consumption of this beverage was common in Yemen. The word coffee comes from the Arab *qahwa*. Towards the middle of the 16th century, Arab traders were the only ones who transported the beans. However, there is a story behind that only the most curious have looked into.

The key is to observe back and forward from the first European reference of the beverage, written by the German doctor Leonard Rauwolf from a trip to Aleppo, in Syria, and published in a travel book in 1582: "A drink so black as ink and remedy to all sorts of ailments. Its consumers take it in the morning in a porcelain jar that passes from hand to hand and from which everyone fills his own glass." Looking back, we find Islamic protagonists that related to the Sufis, Muslim mystics and frequent travelers between the horn of Africa and the south of Arabia. Ethiopian Sufis, as summed up by Santiago Lascasas in his *Biography of coffee*, "discovered the utility of coffee to allow them to stay awake and dedicate themselves to meditation and prayer for whole nights," and adds "presumably they would inform of this beneficial practice for them to their brothers from other lands. The closest were the Sufis of Arabia, specifically the inhabitants of Yemen."

If we look forward a bit but before its dissemination in Europe, we can locate the legend of the goatherd Kaldi,[1] spread in the first instance through the work of Faust Nairone Banesius, De *saluberrima Cahue seu* Café *nuncupata Discursus*, published in Rome in 1671. As Lascasas himself specifies, Narione was "a Syrian maronite monk, professor of oriental

Three thousand five hundred years ago, the members of the tribe of the oromo, might be the first beneficiaries by the attributes of the coffee Bush, the fruit of the coffee was also used as food.

languages in Rome [who] wrote driven by the interest of giving a Christian origin to a beverage of purely Muslim origin." Mark Pendergrast, in his book *The history of coffee and how it transformed our world*, tells that when priests suggested to pope Clement VIII (1592 to 1605) to forbid the "Muslim beverage", the pope exclaimed: "Well, this satanic beverage is so delicious it would be a shame that infidels had its exclusive use. We will cheat Satan by baptizing it and making it an authentic Christian drink." During these times, Mocha, a

---

[1] Legend has it that a goatherd of Arab origin, named Kaldi, walking his goats on the slopes of Kaffa (Ethiopia) realized they became happy and playful after eating the red fruit from a bush. Kaldi tasted the berries and suddenly he was dancing too. This event was known by an imam in Yemen, who apparently was the first to use the beans and prepare a drink that was useful to keep awake during his nocturnal prayers.

Strictness of the 16th century from Constantinople to Egypt there were numerous coffee houses, where Muslims gather to enjoy this brew.

thirty five hundred years ago members of the Oromo tribe may have been the first benefited by the attributes of the coffee bush. And as supported by the historian C. G. H. Schaefer in his article "Coffee Unobserved: Consumption and Commoditization of Coffee in Ethiopia before the Eighteenth Century," the fruit of coffee was also used as food.

With this sharpness and precision with which researchers force us to look at the phenomena of the world, we must clarify that in Kaffa coffee was called, and still is, *bunchum, buna and bun.*

The Oromo tribe was involuntarily the precursor of the dissemination of *bunchum.* Feuding with another tribe, the Bongo, they used to be defeated by warriors that instead of killing them, sold them as slaves in Arab markets. Probably, the custom to feed on products derived from the coffee bush was imitated in places where they were subjected.

The dissemination of this product also brings our gaze back to the Sufis, Muslim mystics "that were searching the direct relationship with God." These religious men that would convert to Islam had a wide network of adepts in the Arab world and contacts with the Eastern world. Without a historical certainty, it has been speculated that this community could mimic the way their Chinese allies prepared tea and adapt this process to make an infusion of coffee. It was the Sufis of Ethiopia the first ones to use its properties to stay awake for several hours praying. From the meetings they had with other mystics in Egypt and these with alchemists in Yemen, coffee would initiate its expansion route.

The first plantations in Yemen towards the 16th century had to answer to a practical sense. It would be easier to collect coffee on the Arabian Peninsula than to transport it from Ethiopia. The stimulating effect that propelled the mystics was then reinterpreted as a recreational activity that even led to a temporary ban. However, its use was so widespread among the Muslim culture that quickly an intervention lifted the ban. Idris Bostan thus summarizes the influence of its market in the 18th century: "The coffee that came from Yemen circulated in Egypt. It arrived to Istanbul through the ports of Damietta, Rosetta and Alexandria."

When telling the story of coffee we also recover its symbolism

port in Yemen, had the commercial monopoly of coffee, brought from Tihama (also in Yemen), the first place where it was systematically cultivated, but it was also sold as a bean in Ethiopia, on occasions of better quality than the Yemeni. At the beginning of the 16th century from Constantinople to Egypt there were multiple coffee houses, where Muslims gathered to enjoy this concoction. European merchants that visited Mocha confirmed the commercial success of the toasted bean, zealously guarded by the Yemenis, making sure that foreigners didn't take fertile beans that they could sow in other lands. Although pope Clement VIII hadn't expressed those words, this saying reflects the discovery of coffee by Europeans who, charmed by its flavor, properties and guarantee as a profitable business, resolved breaking the monopoly that the port of Mocha preserved during 150 years as the solely distributor worldwide. The first to try were the English. The first European Coffee house was installed in London around 1650. While in Venice the first coffee house opened in 1683, something that Antony Wild, in his book *Black Gold: A dark history of coffee*, considers as a historic anomaly, since Venice was considered the commercial bridge between East and West.

But let's go back to where it all began. Stewart Lee Allen, in the novel *The Devil's Cup; coffee, the driving force in history,* transports us to Kaffa, in the southwest of Ethiopia, where

Towards the end of the 16th century, European, intrigued, scientists began to analyze the properties of coffee. Its use was restricted to the elites and for some time it was considered a medicinal drink.

merchandise or by the news about coffee houses that were becoming popular on routes to or returning from Mecca, the grain radiated to all the world thanks to the colonial expansion.

Towards the end of the 16th century, European scientists, intrigued, began to analyze the properties of coffee. Its use was restricted to elites and for a time it was considered as a medicinal drink. It wasn't until the 18th century that its attributes were associated to the development of intellect and the conservation of the vigor to work. Its crescent acceptance gave place to the idea of producing it outside the Arab territory. In France and Holland it was tried to adapt the bush to the botanical gardens. The Dutch were the first to achieve the acclimatization of the coffee tree on land that was not subject to Arab control, moving the seeds to their possessions in Java, in Indonesia. Louis XIV, the sun king, received in 1714 a coffee plant "with the height of a man," gift from the burgomaster of Amsterdam, even a year before the Sultan of Yemen had given him also some plants of the same product in gratitude for the care he received from a French navy doctor. Although Louis XIV, perhaps copying the Dutch strategy, ordered the expansion of coffee tree plantations, his death in 1715 coincided with the arrival of the first plants to the island of Bourbon, east of Madagascar. The Dutch, one step ahead, had moved their

and representation. For example in the Bible, the first book of Samuel, Chapter XXV, verse 18, says: "Abigail hastily took two hundred loaves and two wine skins, five sheep already prepared, five measures of roasted grain, a hundred cakes of raisin and two hundred cakes of dry figs." In some translations, it is established that the five measures were of toasted wheat, but the most spread one leaves to the interpretation of the reader the kind of toasted "grain". In *The Odyssey*, Homer says that Helen of Troy received from Polidamna, Egyptian queen, a plant that when mixed with wine made her forget all of her ailments; several suggested that this plant was the bush of coffee.

Once the West learned about the existence of this product by the stories of its travelers, by the diversion of arab

Louis XIV, the Sun King, received in 1714 a coffee plant "the height of a man", gift of the burgomaster of Amsterdam.

The French Lieutenant Gabriel Mathieu d'Erchigny de Clieu, in 1723, led a plan to America, his target was Martinique, where it spread to the island of Guadalupe.

Clieu, who, according to what is told, had only carried one plant, had greater repercussion in America. His destination was Martinique, from where it spread to the island of Guadalupe, then to Santo Domingo, and then to Haiti, all French colonies, but an uprising of slaves in the latter place gave circumstantially the opportunity to the Spanish to continue the coffee route, because Haiti producers moved with this knowledge to the island of Cuba. For its part, the Portuguese, apparently through not so legitimate means, had removed the seeds from the French Guyana and the island of Bourbon, in order to start crops in Brazil, where they would employ the labor of African slaves. This way, at the beginning of the 19th century, France lost the control of the production on American soil that, it's necessary to clarify, was only used to provide coffee to European consumers, for a full century had to go by for the American people to appreciate the virtues of the beverage that, more than three thousand years before, had been discovered by the Oromo.

crops from Java to Surinam in 1714, in what is considered as the first plantation in America. However, the travel in 1723 of the French lieutenant Gabriel Mathieu d'Erchigny de

EVOLUTION OF COFFEE CONSUMPTION IN THE WORLD

In 1982, UNESCO defined the term culture as "the whole complex of distinctive spiritual, material, intellectual and emotional features that characterize a society or social group". From an anthropological sense, "culture or civilization, in a wide ethnographic sense, is [a] whole complex which includes knowledge, beliefs, art, morals, law, customs and any other capabilities and habits acquired by men as members of a society". Therefore, we can say that there is a culture around coffee, whose history and evolution of the practices of its culture have evolved in a variety of artistic manifestations (painting, sculpture, music, architecture), crafts, science, dance, musical customs, education, gastronomy, government, history, industry, business, agriculture, literature, religion and traditions.[3]

In the book *Coffee, the drink that conquered the world*, it is quoted: "then the young man took a handful of seeds–fruits– prepared an infusion, drank it with delight and a great comfort came over him and he forgot his hardships, he was Ali Ben Omar Al Shadhili, patron of coffee cultivators".[4]

Perhaps at the beginning only the soft pulp around the seed was consumed, until the stimulant properties of coffee were discovered. Then they would eat the composite grains in a paste mixed with animal fats, a fact documented when it is narrated that, since ancient times, the Abyssinians used coffee as a stimulant to support the fatigue and pain produced by the arduous treks through the desert. "They chewed small portions of a paste in a 'cake' made from fresh ground coffee mixed with salted butter or cooked fruits and coffee tree leaves and predictably of roasted beans, harvested from wild and semi-domesticated plants".[6]

The Arabs of the Yemen was who gave the first great boom of coffee, its original preparation was an infusion made with shell, which they called "Kixr" while drinkers fist boiled whole berries.

These stories seem to anticipate events. It is estimated that before the fifteenth century, coffee cherries were chewed only for its toning effects, the practice of turning them into a drink, Tom Standage says, seems to be a Yemeni innovation, often attributed to Muhammad al-Dabani, scholar and member of the Sufi mystic order of Islam who died around 1470.[7]

However, some complement the legend of the goatherd who saw his goats (or camels?) eat the leaves and the fruit of a shrub (in the year 1140), by saying he led them to a convent "where a concoction that was thrown into the fire because

---

[1] Mexico Declaration on cultural policies. World Conference on cultural policies. Organización de las Naciones Unidas para la Educación, la Ciencia y la Cultura (UNESCO), México D. F., 26 de julio al 6 de agosto de 1982.
[2] Definition of E. B. Tylor (*Primitive culture*), included in zz Pelayo García Sierra, Biblioteca Filosofía en español, consulted in http://filosofia.org/filomat.
[3] According to Coltman, M., cited by Berzunza, Gloria, A.C. y Mejía Martínez, N.A. "Puesta en valor del Patrimonio de San Pedro Cholula a través de rutas turísticas", tesis de Licenciatura, UDLAP, 2003, http://catarina.udlap.mx/u.dl.a/tales/documentos/lhr/berzunza_g_ac/capitulo2.pdfs.
[4] Pérez Pérez, Juan Ramón and Salvador Díaz Cárdenas. *El Café, bebida que conquistó al mundo*, México, Universidad Autónoma Chapingo, 2000.
[5] Hernández, Avelino, *op. cit.*
[6] Pérez Pérez, Juan Ramón and Salvador Díaz Cárdenas, *op. cit.*
[7] Standage, Tom. *La historia del mundo en seis tragos. De la cerveza de los faraones a la Coca-Cola*, México, Random House, 2007.

of its bad taste, was prepared. However, from the seeds a sublime aroma escaped, which gave the idea of preparing the beverage with roasted beans" ; or that Kaldi, which was the name of the goatherd, took the cherries to the religious leader of the place who, fearing this was the work of the devil, threw them into the fire where they roasted and released its exquisite aroma, then they were removed form the fire and mixed with water so that everyone had a chance to taste the divine gift.[9]

Of how it arrived to Yemen, main commercialization center for many years and the reason why the origin of coffee was attributed to Arab lands, the most convincing explanation was that the king of Abyssinia, Elesboas or Calab from Axum conquered Yemen in the fourth century and maintained his government for 67 years, enough to think that the use of coffee as a stimulant, either chewed or in infusion, was common on both sides of the Red Sea.[10]

The truth is that Arabs from Yemen where the ones who gave coffee its first boom, its original preparation was an infusion made with the shell, which they called "*Kixr*" ("Kisher", according to other versions), while the first drinkers boiled the whole berries. In Egypt they preferred the husk of the grain. In Yemen they assured that kixr had a better flavor if the husk was fresh, and good drinkers rejected sugar.[11]

Drinkers of that time came to exclaim: "Surely, Allah wanted to compensate us for the prohibition of drinking wine, since man can not always bear the pain and needs relief in difficult times". The name given to the drink was "*Kawa*" which in Arab means, "that which brings joy and lightens the mind".

Bartra, Cobo and Paz[13] relate various ways to consume coffee in the East, one of them is to prepare it without beans and using the dried pulp that covers the seed, it is the so-called

There are people who complement the legend of the pastor who saw his goats (or camels?) eat the leaves and the fruit of a shrub (in the year 1140), leading to a convent "where was prepared a brew that was thrown into the fire for their bad taste.

[8] Conaculta. Culturas Populares. *Recetario del café*, México, Conaculta, 1997, p 14.
[9] Ilario, José, Editor. *La guía Epicur del café, copa y puro*, Epicur Publicaciones, Barcelona, s/f.
[10] Pérez Pérez, Juan Ramón and Salvador Díaz Cárdenas, *op. cit.*, p. 27.
[11] Sierra, pp. 10-11, cited by Bartra Vergés, Armando, *et al., La hora del café. Dos siglos a mucha voces.* México, Comisión Nacional para el Conocimiento y Uso de la Biodiversidad, 2011.
[12] Pérez Pérez, Juan Ramón y Salvador Díaz Cárdenas, *op. cit.*

"Sultana coffee", usually consumed by distinguished Arabs. According to a quote by La Roque, it was prepared as follows: the ripe and fragmented bark and pulp are put to roast over charcoal fire, so they acquire some color; while water boils in a kettle. When the bark is roasted it is thrown in the water so it boils as if it were ordinary coffee. In the court of Yemen, during the visits of governors and people of distinction, this kind of coffee was the only one taken; delicate drink, it is not necessary to add sugar since it contains a natural slight sweetness.

Fakirs drank coffee in the temple, while singing praises to the Lord. From a large glass of red clay, the superior pulled the coffee through a bowl and distributed to each of the fakirs, while singing their regular prayers. Lay brothers and all attendees drank as well.

Pietro della Valle, who lived in Constantinople, refer Bartra, Cobo and Paz, wrote in 1615:

The Turks also have a black colored concoction that during the summer is refreshing, while in winter provides a lot of heat, whose nature, however, remains unchanged and is taken hot in both cases… It is drank in big gulps, not during meals but after, as a kind of delicacy, and also in small sips, to chat at ease in the company of friends. Whenever they get together they take it. To this purpose a big fire is kept alive beside which are placed some small cups of porcelain, full of this liquid, and when it is hot enough, as hot as possible, there are men who serve it to all of those present, and also giving each melon seeds to chew. And with the seeds and this concoction called Cahué, they distract themselves talking… sometimes for seven or eight hours.

This boom was reflected in the fact that by 1570 there were two thousand coffee houses in Cairo, called Kawha-Kanes, where in addition to selling the drink they played chess and the conversations were about prose, verses, arts, science, and very soon they discussed, although timidly, religion and politics.[14]

Drinking big drinks, not during the meal, but then, as a kind of candy, and also in small sips, to talk at easy in the company of friends.

As it has been seen, West travelers gave account of the fashion of coffee in their countries, so it didn't take long for its impact to reach Europe. In 1652 the first coffee houses were established in London; by 1715 this capital already had about two thousand cafés that were also centers of gathering for social, political, literary and commercial life.

When the first café was created in London, it was advertised as follows in a flyer (the original is kept in the British Museum):
The virtues of coffee made and sold publicly by
Pasqua Rosse

[13] Bartra Vergés, Armando, *et al.*, pp 46-50.
[14] Pérez Pérez, Juan Ramón and Salvador Díaz Cárdenas, *op. cit.*

The grain or fruit called coffee is produced by a shrub that grows in the deserts of Arabia. Boiled with water after its virtues have been dried and reduced to powder, it makes a simple and innocent drink suitable to be taken one hour after a meal... It animates the spirit and strengthens the heart; it removes headaches; it is excellent to prevent and cure gout and dropsy. In Turkey, where this drink is common, it has been observed that nobody suffers from stones, also (they have) clear, smooth and white skin...[15]

The arrival of coffee to France brought the addition of sugar to the drink. José Lozada Tomé[16] states that it was in 1659 when the drink appeared in Paris through the visit of Saliman Aga as ambassador of the Sultan of Turkey. Guests of the ambassador were served coffee, and although he says "it was served adding sugar following their custom," Salvador Novo tells it his way: "nobles began to send their ladies, intrigued by a lively curiosity and willing to pay to see such a

In 1652 established the first cafes in London; 1715 this capital had already nearly two thousand cafes were simultaneously meeting social, political, literary and commercial life centers.

strange wonder, the price of absorbing coffee. A Viscountess pretended to go give a sweet to the caged birds of the strange room, and dropped it into her cup of coffee. Saliman did not seem to notice, but the following day, his slaves offered, with coffee, sugar cubes to the ladies.[17]

An interesting story of 1782 allows us to see how the drink quickly became popular in Paris:

The most moving sight is perhaps offered by the street vendors, in the corners, when the laborers go to work, at day break: they carry on their backs a tin container and they serve coffee with milk in bowls of clay for two salaries. Sugar is not abundant... Success, however, is huge; laborers have found this food cheaper and... more full of flavor than any other. Consequently, they drink it in prodigious amounts and they say it helps them to keep standing on their feet until nighttime.[18]

As in Asia, in Europe coffee also provoked that the places where it was served became meeting points to debate, analyze, and assume political positions, which in many occasions caused governments of both continents to close these places. In France the taste for coffee was highlighted: "Paris becomes a great café. Never has there been so many conversations and so spiritual", José Lozada tells us in his essay "Something about coffee in the world",[19] getting ahead of an interesting interpretation of Tom Standage.

In fact, Standage refers that coffee was the dominant drink in the "Age of reason" and he stresses that the establishments that began to serve coffee were very different from taverns that sold alcoholic drinks, the former becoming centers of commercial, political and intellectual exchange. "Coffee –he affirms– encouraged clarity of thought, so it was the ideal drink for scientists, businessmen and philosophers. Coffee gatherings led to the founding of scientific societies, journals

[15] Gómez G., 1894. *Cultivo y beneficio del café*, p. 32, cited in Pérez Pérez, Juan Ramón and Salvador Díaz Cárdenas, *op. cit.*
[16] "Algo sobre el café en el mundo", en *Artes de México*, núm 192, año XXII. El café en México, 1978.
[17] Novo, Salvador. *Cocina mexicana o historia de la gastronómica de la ciudad de México*, México, Editorial Porrúa, 1967, cited in *La hora del café. Dos siglos a mucha voces, op. cit.*, p. 26.
[18] Braudel, Fernand. *Bebidas y excitantes*, México, Alianza Cien, Conaculta, 1994 citado en Bartra Vergés, Armando, *et al., op. cit.*, p. 44.
[19] Published in *Artes de México, op. cit.*

and economic institutions, and provided a fertile ground to the revolutionary thought, especially in France."[20]

Standage attributes the change of the taste for beer and wine to coffee because the latter allowed to start the day lucid and stimulated thus improving the result of work; moreover, if people resorted to beer and wine because it was deemed safer than water, which was likely contaminated "especially in miserable and overpopulated cities", with coffee the problem was solved in a better way.

To the term Age of Reason, Standage adds the term "drink of reason", to which many creators coincide. Balzac, for instance, writes a eulogy to coffee:

When coffee falls into your stomach, everything becomes agitated; ideas quick-march into motion like battalions of a great army in the fighting ground; the battle begins. Memories charge in, bright flags on high. The cavalry deploys a magnificent gallop. The artillery of logic rushes up

[20]Standage, Tom, *op. cit.*, p. 16.

Standage attributed to the change of taste for beer and wine into coffee, because this allowed start the day lucid and stimulated, thus improving the result of the work.

On the subject that Voltaire drank more than twenty cups a day, Fernando Savater comments, "he achieved his insomnia to be perpetual". To the criticism over his addiction, Voltaire himself answered: "of course coffee is a slow poison, I have been drinking it for forty years.[22]

Regarding the best way to brew coffee at the time of the encyclopedists, Brillat-Savarin wrote in Physiology of taste, his "ninth meditation" to boast not who discovered it, but who thought about roasting it "decoction of raw coffee is an insignificant drink, but its carbonization develops an aroma and forms an oil that characterizes coffee the way we drink it". Between ground and crushed coffee he says he prefers the latter and suggests as the best way to prepare it "the Dubilloy," which "consists of pouring boiling water over the coffee previously put on a porcelain or silver glass, fitted with small holes. This first decoction is taken and heated to a boiling point, it is strained once more; and the best possible light coffee is obtained."[23]

To the United States it arrived from 1670, according to the first selling license, which was given to a woman –Dorothy Jones-. In less than 20 years there were cafés in Boston, New York and Philadelphia, among the main cities.

In 1711, a Japanese invented instant coffee, or soluble coffee, which was used by the US army in 1918, near the end of the war. The innovation ceased to be interesting until it was launched to the market by a perfumer of New York in 1939, but it was until 1945 that it became commercially imposed.[24]

with clattering wagons and cartridges. Mental occurrences act as handles in combat. Figures of thought put on their best clothes, the paper is filled with ink, the battle reaches its climax and ends between rivers of black currents, just as an authentic battle drowning in the black smoke of gunfire.[21]

[21] Bartra Vergés, Armando, *et al.*, p. 38.
[22] http://www.proverbia.net/citastema.asp?tematica=671.
[23] E. Deschamps R. "Desde México y en busca de la biografía del cafeto", in *Artes de México, op. cit.*
[24] Sierra Partida, cited by Bartra Vergés, Armando, *et al., op. cit.*, p. 22.

ITS ARRIVAL TO MEXICO

ITS ARRIVAL TO MEXICO

The taste for coffee, the possibility of producing it and distributing it, caused the coffee plant to be taken, since the 17th century, to the French, English, Dutch, Portuguese and Spanish colonies in America.

The spread of crops around the world had peaked in the 18th century, when the essential knowledge about the type of soil, climate and agricultural processes for sowing, care, harvest, grain processing, packaging and distribution were dominated. The first plants arrived from Cuba to New Spain in the last few years of the 18th century to be sown on farms in Cordoba, Veracruz.

The accuracy of the year of arrival is not known with precision. There are records that place it in 1740, but another source states the year of 1784 and even mentions that it was José Antonio Selebert who introduced them. Other authors say it was in 1790, one more in 1796, some fix the date in 1800 and some even until 1804. Those who located the arrival amid the end of a century and the beginning of the next, coincide that it was Juan Antonio Gómez de Guevara, count of Oñate, who introduced coffee through seeds obtained in Havana, Cuba, to propagate them in his Hacienda of Guadalupe, located near the city of Cordoba, Veracruz.

Doubts about the arrival of coffee to Mexico are due both to a Royal Order issued by the imperial government of Spain in 1790 —which exempted from taxes on coffee and sugar sent to the capital of the kingdom- as to the precise data of Alexander von Humboldt who stated that at the beginning of the 19th century the exportations of New Spain were 360 hundredweights of coffee annually. This data is complemented with the records of the products exported through the port of Veracruz during the years 1802, 1803 and 1805, which include coffee with 272, 493 and 336 hundredweights respectively.

Seeds that were planted in Coatepec also came from Cuba. Historians of this city specify that it was exactly on May 16, 1808, when the Spanish José Arias brought them, while the presbyter José Santiago Contreras and the parish priest Andrés Domínguez were in charge of planting them. In 1809 the first plantation was made in the city of Xalapa.

This year the culture started in Cuernavaca and Yautepec with 400 thousand coffee trees by Jaime Salvet, a Spanish established in these places and frequently remembered because of a letter he sent to the viceroy of New Spain, Pedro of Garibay, on March 6, 1809, in which he asked for tax exemption and the payment of tithe for 25 years. The petition was denied under the argument that there were already coffee plantations in Agualulcos, Oaxaca.

From the first plantations, the crops spread to several nearby areas, as Huatusco and the Zongolica sierra, in addition to other more distant: Huautla, Chinantla and the now called Juarez sierra in Oaxaca. From these plantations they expanded to Puebla, the State of Mexico, San Luis Potosí and Guerrero.

The precision of the year of arrival is not known with accuracy. There are records that placed it in 1740, but another source sets the year of 1784 and even mentions that it was José Antonio Selebert who introduces them.

A second shipment of coffee plants arrived to the African island of Mauritius. General José Mariano Michelena, lieutenant of the Infantry Regimen of the Spanish Crown, switched sides to the supporters of the independence, where he became plenipotentiary of Guadalupe Victoria and, as part of his duties, traveled to Europe, Asia and Africa.

From the port of Mocha, Michelena brought coffee plants that he acclimatized in his hacienda La Parota, located in Ziracuaretiro, near Uruapan, Michoacán. Once again the dates overlap. Some say it was in 1823; one more that in 1828, and to avoid errors, some speak of "the twenties" of the 19th century, although other authors point out that it was in 1838 and some more that in the thirties.

It is believed that this was the starting point for the dissemination of the culture in the states of Colima, Jalisco and Nayarit.

In Oaxaca the cultivation dates back to the early 18th century, with plants coming from Cordoba, Veracruz, and they were planted in the atrium of the church of San Pedro Piña in Pochutla. Over the years a shift in the production of cochineal, which was used as a colorant, occurred, but due to the emergence of aniline, demand decreased; for this reason coffee cultivation was favored and many families were dedicated to this work in the district of Pochutla, the same that would lead to the birth of the municipality of Pluma Hidalgo.

Another record of coffee cultivation in Oaxaca points out that José María Cortés, parish priest of the church of San Agustín, made the first crop in Loxicha in 1854.
The third route of arrival of coffee to Mexico was from Guatemala. In 1846 the Italian Jerome Manchinelli installed an experimental plantation of fifteen hundred coffee trees brought from San Pablo de Guatemala, to his farm "La Chácara", in Tuxtla Chico, Chiapas.

Afterwards, as of 1871, Carlos Gris, from Zacatecas, would allocate his state "Majahual", located in the cacao zone of Cacahotan, to the cultivation of coffee. In ten years he planted 100 thousand coffee trees. Thus, the Soconusco started to be involved in coffee production, where Spanish missionaries, that also promoted the culture, arrived. In addition, German farmers from Guatemala settled in Soconusco, in the town now called Unión Juárez, bringing with them coffee trees for cultivation.

Little by little coffee cultivation zones were formed in Mexico; the entities where they developed the most were Veracruz, Chiapas and Oaxaca. In others, the development was smaller, like in Puebla, Tabasco, Nayarit, Hidalgo, Michoacán, Colima, Jalisco and Guerrero. All of this happened without specific plans to promote coffee cultivation. Something Alexander Von Humboldt himself had suggested to exploit the soil and climate of Mexico, "extraordinarily favorable for coffee cultivation," more profitable and easier than sugar cane and with less investment.

The commercialization expectations of the grain influenced the spread of its crops, although mainly for the export market. Let's recall that the first shipment of this product abroad was recorded in 1802. From 1850, and for the following forty years, plantations spread across the slopes of the Pacific and Gulf of Mexico, specifically in areas of central and northern Veracruz, in the Sierra Norte of Puebla, on the south coast of Oaxaca, in the Hidalgo and San Luis Potosi Huasteca, in some middle elevations of Tabasco, in the Highlands region, Soconusco and Northern Sierra of Chiapas, as well as smaller sites of entities like Michoacán, Guerrero, Colima, Nayarit and Jalisco.

Of the first plantations spread cultivation to several nearby areas such as Huatusco and the Sierra de Zongolica, in addition to other more distant: Huautla, la Chinantla and the so-called now Sierra Juárez, Oaxaca.

Coffee plantation pawns. Photography taken in 1906

The rise in the international demand for coffee motivated the impulse and proliferation of its cultivation in Mexico. Suffice it to recall the tax exemption promoted by the Royal Order of the Government of Spain in 1790 and the registration of export from the port of Veracruz in the early 19th century. The independent movement and the subsequent political instability delayed the growth and proliferation of coffee plantations, however, Mexican and foreign farmers continued with the start and expansion of their plantations.

The political reorganization during the Juarez government allowed some conditions and guarantees –through a social policy with immigration, small property and free labor objectives- for the development of coffee production with domestic and foreign capital.

Coupled with the purpose of promoting the cultivation of coffee, there was a need to colonize spacious grounds with tropical and semi-tropical climates suitable for this crop. Through legislation, executive orders and various promotions, it was sought to attract European, North-American settlers and all those with means to invest in the Mexican countryside. Although since before there had been a significant migration of German coffee growers from Guatemala to Soconusco, this environment generated the production boom since 1870 and it would remain beyond the long period of government of Porfirio Díaz.

The investment in coffee plantations was both from national as well as from foreign capital (Italian, Spanish, German.) From the German investment a singular case stands out, that of Karl Sartorius, who had come to Mexico since the 1820s with the idea of founding a German colony in a free place without arbitrary authorities and where conditions would ensure economic, cultural and even ideological survival. By the end of that decade he bought the hacienda El Mirador, located in Huatusco, between Xalapa and Orizaba, where he experimented growing plants such as potatoes, pineapple, sugar cane and coffee, although until then the analysis of these crops had not been systematized.

In 1850, Sartorius and his family used water to remove the grain cover, thus initiating a modest coffee agro-industry.

Production and commercialization of Mexican coffee

Once coffee was introduced to the areas that would propel the geography of coffee in Mexico in the second half of the 19th century, capitalism entered rural areas through the implementation of agricultural products with commercial values for the metropolis.

Washing tanks. Photography taken in 1906

Political and social control of the porfiriato contributed to that in the last decade of the 19th century of high production levels to reach.

With the gathered information he wrote and made known 16 monographic articles about coffee tree cultivation, related to coffee areas in the states of Chiapas: *Coffee cultivation in Soconusco* (1874) and *Coffee on the southern coast of Chiapas* (1875); Veracruz: *Coffee cultivation in Cordoba Canton, Coffee cultivation in Jalacingo Canton, Coffee cultivation in Orizaba Canton* and *Coffee cultivation in Huatusco Canton* (1879); Jalisco: *Coffee cultivation in Jalisco* (1877); Colima: *Coffee cultivation in Colima* (1877) and Michoacán: *Coffee cultivation in Michoacán* and *Coffee of Uruapan* (1877).

Of special mention is Oaxaca, his home state, to which he dedicated Coffee cultivation in the state of Oaxaca; *Coffee cultivation in the districts of Teotitlán and Tuxtepec*, Oaxaca; *Coffee cultivation in the district of Choapan*, Oaxaca; *Coffee cultivation in the districts of Villa Alta and Villa Juárez*, Oaxaca; *Coffee cultivation in the district of Miahuatlán*, Oaxaca; *Coffee cultivation in the district of Juquila, Oaxaca*, and *Coffee cultivation in the district of Pochutla, Oaxaca, all of them between 1880 and 1881.*

Small-scale production soon became large plantations whose production was destined for the world market and was controlled by German, British an US companies. This was helped by the increase of international coffee prices in 1888 because of a significant reduction in production in Brazil due to political instability, in addition that in Mexico the production was increasing in large parts of Oaxaca.

The political and social control of the Porfirio Diaz period helped to reach high levels of production in the last decade of the 19th century. From 1826 to 1895, the number of coffee plants in Mexico went from 500 thousand to 25 million coffee trees in production and an estimated 50 million more had been planted in four years (1891-1895).

In this period, Mexican coffee production gained prominence and even transformed large regions of Veracruz, Chiapas and Oaxaca.

The writings of Matías Romero about coffee production in various regions of the country give an account of this. Matías Romero also reported the different types of terrain, the density of the coffee plantations, the particular experiences of the coffee producers in terms of investment, production and profits, along with various facts about the introduction and development of coffee cultivation in each region.

He also integrated two large monographs on the subject, published in the form of books. The one titled *Coffee cultivation in the Mexican Republic* reprinted on several occasions, as was another one with the name *Coffee and India rubber culture in Mexico* that aimed to spread in the United States the importance of Mexican coffee.

The production of coffee was starting its path towards technification, to which contributed German coffee farms that, with their historical, statistical, economic and migratory records spread out from Guatemala to Mexico, specifically to Soconusco, as told in his apology to this farms by Manuel Efrén López Echeverría:

The specificity of the study is to highlight the importance of introducing the analysis and composition of the soil, to be clear about orographic differences, the most convenient fertilizer, the growth of the plant, how much performance can be obtained from each plant; that is, there is standardization. It's not just about the analysis of the composition of the soil, but a whole series of variables that ultimately have to do with the production of coffee, for the standardization of the production, to obtain a stable type of coffee, a type of standard seed of the same size, the same weight, to be able to even assign tasks to the workers to know how much coffee can be obtained from each plant, to make a yearly estimate of how much it can be produced and how much can be offered on the market, what will be the gain and when will this gain be available for reinvestment or to purchase machinery, electricity. A calculation made only by them, this is called standardization of coffee.

With the same seriousness it is described how to replace one of the production factors: "Due to lack of manpower, in 1897, for heavy work on farms 400 Jamaican black slaves and kanaka Indians from Polynesia, who died slowly, were imported."

The Soconusco was characterized by the quality of their coffee, but Veracruz was the state with the highest production during the Porfiriato, followed by Colima, Chiapas, Guerrero, Michoacán, Morelos, Oaxaca and Tabasco. Cultivation then spread to Jalisco, Tamaulipas, Durango, state of Mexico, Nayarit, Sinaloa and Coahuila.

As an export product, the production was subject to the international market fluctuations and the domestic market was destined only 31% of production. On coffee farms there were small plantations with low technology and abundant cheap labor, whose fruit had to go through the landowners for its processing and commercialization, with which the collection of grain destined to the international market was ensured.

The rise in the production was reflected between 1888 and 1897 when Mexican coffee producers increased their exports by 400%, from 80 thousand to 400 thousand 60 kg bags, taking advantage as well of the rising prices.

The period of the Mexican Revolution did not reflect damages on coffee production. With minimum care for the plantations, harvesting time and everyday life continued, to be disturbed only when armed groups broke into the region. The grain continued to be exported: from 1911 to 1915 a volume close to 1.93 million bags was sold abroad, mainly to the United States (72.4% of the total). From 1910 to 1920, 675 thousand bags were produced.

Drying coffee parchment. Photography taken in 1908

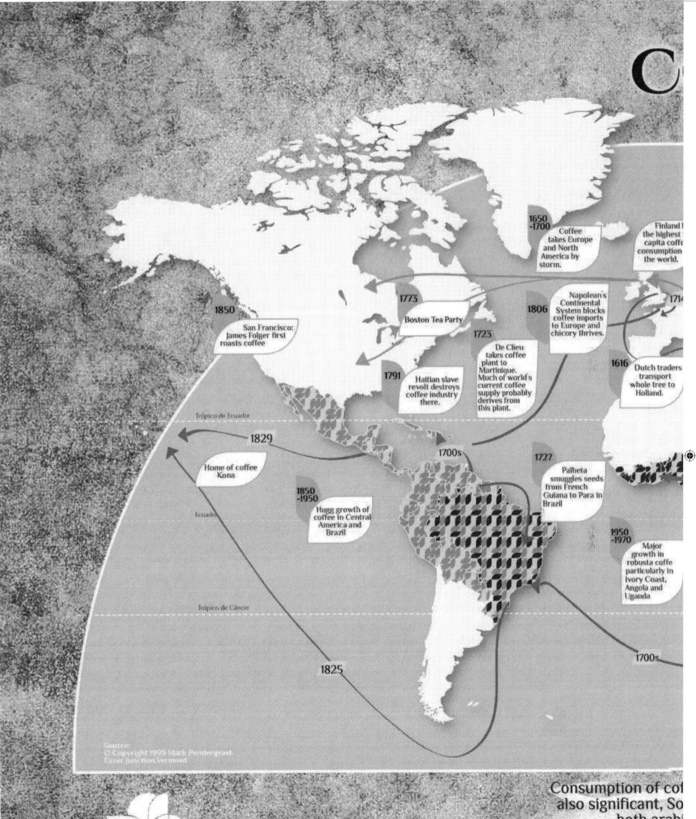

C

1650-1700 Coffee takes Europe and North America by storm.

Finland [has] the highest [per] capita coffee consumption [in] the world.

1773 Boston Tea Party

1850 San Francisco: James Folger first roasts coffee

1723 De Clieu takes coffee plant to Martinique. Much of world's current coffee supply probably derives from this plant.

1806 Napolean's Continental System blocks coffee imports to Europe and chicory thrives.

1714

1791 Haitian slave revolt destroys coffee industry there.

1616 Dutch traders transport whole tree to Holland.

1829

Trópico de Ecuador

Home of coffee Kona

1850-1950 Hugg growth of coffee in Central America and Brazil

Ecuador

1700s

1727 Palheta smuggles seeds from French Guiana to Para in Brazil

1950-1970 Major growth in robusta coffe particularly in Ivory Coast, Angola and Uganda

Trópico de Cáncer

1825

1700s

CAFÉ DE MÉXICO

Consumption of cof[fee]
also significant, So[uth]
both arabi[ca]
ac[]
Consumption arr[]

OFFEE MIGRATION

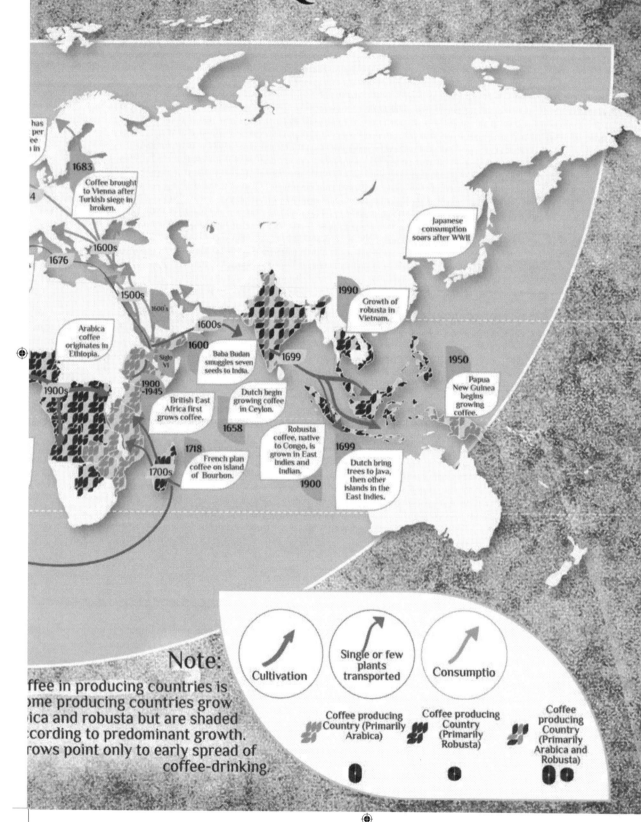

1683 — Coffee brought to Vienna after Turkish siege in broken.

Japanese consumption soars after WWII

1990 — Growth of robusta in Vietnam.

1600s

1676

1500s

1600s

1600s

Arabica coffee originates in Ethiopia.

Siglo VI

1600 — Baba Budan smuggles seven seeds to India.

1699

1950 — Papua New Guinea begins growing coffee.

1900 -1945 — British East Africa first grows coffee.

Dutch begin growing coffee in Ceylon. **1658**

Robusta coffee, native to Congo, is grown in East Indies and Indian. **1900**

1699 — Dutch bring trees to Java, then other islands in the East Indies.

1900s

1718 — French plan coffee on island of Bourbon.

1700s

Note:

ffee in producing countries is
me producing countries grow
ica and robusta but are shaded
cording to predominant growth.
rows point only to early spread of
coffee-drinking.

Cultivation

Single or few plants transported

Consumptio

Coffee producing Country (Primarily Arabica)

Coffee producing Country (Primarily Robusta)

Coffee producing Country (Primarily Arabica and Robusta)

Coffee consumption in Mexico

From the beginning the consumption per capita in Mexico was very limited. At the beginning of the 19th century, Humboldt told in his writings about this situation and he made the comparison that in our country only 400 to 500 hundredweights of coffee were consumed, while in France, with a population five times larger than that of New Spain, close to 230 thousand hundredweights were consumed.

However, and in spite of competing with chocolate and other traditional beverages, it is documented that since 1789 there were already establishments where coffee was enjoyed, first it was offered in ice-cream parlors, pubs, taverns or wine shops, then emerged the creation of specific spaces that became meeting places, headquarters of political clubs and literary circles, among others. In the first decade of the 19th century, with the prior effervescence to the independence movement, these were the places where politics and other social matters were discussed; an account of this is given by *El Diario de México*, that, in its April 17, 1810 issue published the sonnet "Coffee social gathering," which ends with the following verses:

> To talk about religion with little faith,
> and ultimately a good consort berate,
> are the daily gatherings of coffee

Workers of Chiapas. Photography taken in 1935

At the beginning of independent Mexico, cafés proliferated, in these places politics were discussed and they served as meeting places for various social classes, as narrated by several authors, such as the one who wrote under the pseudonym "Argos" in the newspaper El Sol, telling that in the so-called "Cafés" they played dominoes, triplet, chess and in some they would even install bowling and billiards. Some years later these would be greatly criticized by the press, as several of these places where located near the National Preparatory School in San Ildefonso, generating distraction among young scholars.

Other authors that tell their experiences and observations on the cafés of the time where Guillermo Prieto in his "Memories of my times" (1828-1840); Juan Díaz Covarrubias in his work "The middle class" (1858); Manuel Payno in his hovel "The devil's tie pin" (1859), Fernando Orozco y Berra in his article "Breakfast magazine. Progress at dawn" (1851), where he reviews where do people in the capital have their breakfast and what they eat according to their social class.

Although there were some detractors of coffee, there were also people who conferred great benefits upon it, as well as those who offered substitutes for people to whom real coffee was harmful, as the "Legitimate homeopathic coffee" and "Sweet acorn coffee", which were promoted as pleasant, healthy and tonic coffees, for sale in the Chocolate factory "Flower of Tabasco."

At the time of the French intervention and the brief period of the empire of Maximilian of Hapsburg (1864-1867), much of the cafés continued their activities, some changed names and owners. The influence of French manners stood out. French, Austrian and Belgian soldiers joined the regular. Indeed it is a French man who testifies the vision his visit to these cafés left him, the "Café del Hotel Iturbide" of which he recalls the assistance of French soldiers, Italian artists, fortune-seekers from New York and Russia, Polish adventurers, Austrians committed to their emperor, military contractors and other foreigners, in addition to Mexicans boasting dubious military positions.

Upon returning to the republic, with the arrival of Benito Juárez to the capital, social customs did not vary much, many of them where frenchified.

At the beginning of the independent Mexico proliferated cafes, places where discussed policy and served as meeting for different social classes.

As in the previous period, the establishments where you could taste the delicious coffee remained buoyant; but while coffee was served, there was also food and other beverages, apart from the fact that in their names the word "café" was always included: "Café del Bazar (Café Bazaar)," "Gran Café de las Escalerillas (Great Café of the ladders)," "Café Nacional (National Café)," "Café del Progreso (Progress Café)," "Café de la unión (Union Café)," "Café del Cazador (Hunter's Café)," "Café y Restaurant Parisien (Parisian Café and Restaurant)," "Café de Fulcheri (Fulcheri's Café)," "Café de la Concordia (Concord Café)," and even "El Café Cantante (The Singing Café)." *The new guide to Mexico in English, French and Spanish*, edited in 1882, announced 44 cafés.

The frenchifying deepened during the long Porfirian government and, therefore, so did the same customs but now more exacerbated among the aristocracy who fathered the dictatorship, which had among its main symbols of progress and modernity the Paseo de la Reforma, where "Café Colón" opened its doors in 1889.

In Mexico there are news, though inaccurate, that the first coffee shop was installed in 1785;[1] as the taste for chocolate prevailed, it took some time for the taste of coffee to be accepted. Salvador Novo affirmed that the union of milk

and coffee happened until the end of the 18th century due to the frenchified behavior of the high society, as quoted by Clementina Díaz y de Ovando, [2] but she relates that besides formally installed coffees there were street cafés in the corners "high-class cafés, and medium class ones where families attended with their offspring."

Just as it had happened in Europe and Asia, cafés in Mexico were also places where conservatives and liberals discussed political problems; at the same time they drank *fósforos* and *fosforitos* (equal parts of coffee and liquor.) [3]

At the beginning of independent life cafés proliferated, where, according to Manuel Payno, biscuits, toast and *molletes,* coffee and chocolate were offered from the counter, as well as liqueurs and ice cream. A more contemporary author, Enrique Fernández Ledezma, in *Journey to the nineteenth century*, mentions that the café "Veroly" served different types of pastries, and three-part chocolate (with equal parts of cacao, sugar and cinnamon), coffee with vanilla cream, *Pajarete* or *Málaga, Lisia liqueur,* the *Perfect love, Siropped Anise, Cariñera.*

As the 19th century went by, the taste for coffee was consolidated in Mexico but without achieving general acceptance since, as it has been mentioned, neither before nor now the consumption in our country has been widespread. What has been recognized is the quality of the aromatic produced in several parts of the country. In 1873 the protestant pastor Gilbert Haven made the following recommendation:

Mexican coffee is one of the best in the world; the best grain of Colima, on the west coast, is sold at one and a half pesos a pound. It is prepared very strong then served with two thirds of hot milk if you are not used to drinking it. When wanted, the portion of milk disappears until it is only coffee. For the coffee of the house the boys always bring two pots, one with coffee and the other one with milk, and serve to taste. [4]

[1] E. Deschamps R. *op. cit.*
[2] "Díaz y de Ovando, Clementina. "Los cafés del siglo XIX en México", in Artes de México, núm. 192, año XXII, El café en México, 1978.
[3] *Ibidem.*
[4] Haven, Gilbert, "Nuestro vecino de al lado. Un invierno en México", in *Cien viajeros en Veracruz. Crónicas y relatos*, tomo VI, 1856-1874, México, Gobierno del Estado de Veracruz, 1992, cited in Bartra Vergés, Armando, *et al.*

The writers were happy with the ambience of the cafés, of which they praised their peace, the good behavior, seriousness, the distraction of the readings and the meditation achieved through games, unlike premises where wine was served because in them there is trouble, intemperate sentences, and explosion of violent passions and drunkenness. Coffee, instead, is the favorite beverage of mathematicians, astronomers, philosophers, historians, naturalists, diplomats and tradesmen. [5]

Caffee shop La Casa de las Muñecas, Puebla. Photography taken in 1900

The nutritional virtues were stated by the journal *El Progreso de México* that in 1896 published that an infusion of 100 grams of coffee in one pound of water is 100 grams of nutrients. The coffee infusion, it said, appeases hunger and sustains and increases strength when the beverage does not disturb the temperament with its effects or when it is not medically contraindicated.

This journal, as well as the *Bulletin of the Mexican Agricultural Society*, carry out a constant and positive diffusion of the real and supposed virtues of coffee in the late nineteenth century, possibly due to the influence of Matías Romero who, as we have seen, was a great promoter of coffee cultivation in Mexico.

In 1883 the *Bulletin of the Mexican Agricultural Society* spread the use of coffee residues to destroy insects that attack plants in gardens and orchards; in 1886 it told about the virtues of coffee to heal wounds and in 1897 it states that a cup of coffee may be used even as a barometer.

El Progreso de México, for its part, in 1896 announced the discovery of instant coffee; that pure coffee, taken on an empty stomach, is the best protection against infectious diseases; that water used when removing the pulp can be used to make good spirits.

According to more contemporary comments, coffee continues to be more appreciated, against harmful effects of alcohol, because it does not stupefy like alcohol, it doesn't stain like tobacco, it's not dangerous like cocaine, nor tasteless like Coca Cola. [6]

---

[5] Losada Tomé, José. "Algo sobre el café en el mundo", *in Artes de México, op. cit.*
[6] Sierra Partida, Alfonso, *El café y los cafés*, México, Ediciones Cafés Literarios, 1966, cited in Bartra Vergés, Armando, *et al.*

INSTITUTIONALIZATION OF MEXICAN COFFEE GROWING

In Mexico, the promotion and government regulation of coffee growing have gone through several stages. Towards the end of the eighteenth century, the Spanish crown considered the grain as another product extracted from its colonies. The first news of taxes date back to 1790, when the peninsular government issued a Royal Order that exempted tax payment to those who sent coffee and sugar to the capital of the kingdom.[1] Although in 1809 Pedro de Garibay, viceroy of New Spain, denied the request of Jaime Salvet, Spanish who introduced the rubiaceae to Yautepec, Morelos, to be exempt from the payment of tithes for 25 years, on the grounds of promoting the cultivation of 400 coffee plants.[2]

At the time of the independence, however, there was a long period of exemption of taxes, tithes and sales taxes, in addition to bonuses for coffee farmers, in order to foster the increase of plantations. This tax advantages to various farm products applied from 1823 to 1861, as reported in the "Decree. Exemption of all rights to certain fruits of the country," of the Mexican legislation:

> Decree of October 8, 1823, about the exemption of all rights to certain fruits of the country.- The new plantations of coffee, cacao, vineyards and olive trees, and the silk harvested in the country are free of sales tax, tithes and any other right, regardless of their denomination, for ten years.
> On February 27, 1834, the exemption for ten years is corroborated from this date on.
> On October 13, 1843, the freedom granted to coffee is extended for ten more years, in response to the nascent state of this branch of the industry, which for various circumstances has not acquired the increase it is susceptible of. And on October 1853 the pardon is granted for another five years, so in 1861 the product is indefinitely exempted from sales tax.[3]

In the late 19th century, coffee exports yield great benefits to farmers and especially to exporters. In a chronicle of Guillermo Prieto about a trip to Jalapa, Veracruz, the Mexican poet and politician retakes a talk he had with the Coyula family in 1875, from where descriptions of the characteristics of the cultivated fields and the costs of hundredweights are recuperated:

- There are cultivated fields in twenty ranches and haciendas and in the vicinity of Córdoba 20 000 000 plants. They produced 50 000 hundredweights. Cost of each hundredweight, seven pesos. Total value $600 000. Total Cost $350 000. Profit $250 000.
- … the canton of Orizaba, in around 18 negotiations between ranches and haciendas. Number of plants, 2 604 200. Yield $6 510.50. Cost of hundredweight, seven. Total Value $78 126. Total Cost $45 573.50. Profit $32 552.50.
- … In the cantons of Córdoba and Orizaba, there are 22 604 200 coffee plants that leave a Profit of $282 552.50, in spite of the imperfect media of culture…[4]

Later, the government of Díaz imposed in 1893-1894 a tax on exports that until 1897-1898 produced an annual income of 700 thousand pesos to the public funds. The year 1896 marked the beginning of a decline in the international price. Producers reacted demanding a reduction in the fee. The government granted the petition and once again the exports were exempted from taxes.[5]

However, towards the decade of 1930, new economic factors promoted for local, state and federal taxes to the exports to mean 25% of the costs of exporting producers, which generated numerous complaints and encouraged the

[1] See Hernández-Martínez, Gerardo and Susana Córdova Santamaría, *México, café y productores: historia de la cultura cafetalera que transformó nuestras regiones, Coatepec-Chapingo*, Centro Agroecológico del Café A. C., Universidad Autónoma Chapingo, 2011.
[2] See "El Café en México", in *Artes de México*, núm. 192, año XXII, El café en México, 1978.
[3] Cited in Bartra Vergés, et al., *La hora del café. Dos siglos a mucha voces*. México, Comisión Nacional para el Conocimiento y Uso de la Biodiversidad, 2011, p. 169.
[4] Cited in Bartra Vergés, et al., *La hora del café. Dos siglos a mucha voces*. México, Comisión Nacional para el Conocimiento y Uso de la Biodiversidad, 2011, pp. 63-64.
[5] *Idem*, pp 171-172.

creation, in 1937, of the Permanent Commission of Coffee Producers of the Mexican Republic, with the participation of coffee associations from Chiapas, Veracruz and Oaxaca. This organization did not have much success and 12 years later (in 1949) was renewed as the National Agricultural Union of Coffee Producers (UNAC) mainly dedicated to manage the reduction or elimination of state and federal taxes.

By then, the federal government moved in the formation of institutions that would allow it to have more presence in the market, both internal and external. On June 8, 1937, the National Foreign Exchange Bank (BANCOMEXT) was created and on September 1st of the same year, the Mexican Export and Import Company, S. A. (CEIMSA). CEIMSA operated as a commercial subsidiary of BANCOMEXT and from 1939 it participated as a commission agent receiving and distributing regionally industrialized coffee at low prices through its own stores. In 1942 CEIMSA founded the company Cafés de Tapachula, S. de R. L. y C. V., whose function was selling the coffee production of Chiapas and, ultimately, it was responsible for commercializing 60% of the national production. Together with BANCOMEXT, Cafés de Tapachula administered coffee farms owned by Germans, guarded by the government when the country got involved in World War II.[6]

Another government company that took commercialization functions, besides carrying out pre-industrialization activities of the grain, was Mexican Benefits of Coffee (BEMEX), established in 1945.

During the Lázaro Cárdenas administration (1934-1940) coffee farms were expropriated to be distributed among *ejidatarios*. Consequently, by 1940 almost half of the surface cultivated with coffee corresponded to *ejido* lands.[7]

In the administration of Manuel Ávila Camacho (1940-1946) a direct intervention in coffee producing areas was exercised in the heat of World War II. On June 11, 1942, by presidential decree, 77 farms in Chiapas, three in Oaxaca and an important coffee processing plant located in Orizaba, Veracruz, which all belonged to German citizens, were constituted as state property through a trust. Some farms in Chiapas were occupied until July 1943, such as El Refugio and El Portillo; Génova, Morelia and San Enrique in Tapachula; La Independencia and Las Maravillas in Huehuetán.

When the war ended in 1945, most of the farms were returned to their previous owners, who even were compensated.[8]

On October 17, 1949, under the decree of creation of the National Coffee Commission, a public policy towards the coffee sector was initiated. This Commission had the task of improving plantations with the use of modern and adequate cultivation and processing systems in order to increase performance and reduce costs; also it had to organize scientific research in experimental fields, as well as manage credit lines for coffee growers.[9]

The Commission included representatives from the ministries of finance, Agriculture and Livestock, and National Economy, CEIMSA and the National Association of Coffee Producers, which a few days later would become UNAC.[10]

To promote the domestic market, the National Coffee Commission (CONACAFE) in 1955 incorporated to its functions the management of BEMEX, thus consolidating its relationship with small farmers to sell their production. The international presence in forums and coffee organizations also came under their responsibility.

During its five first years, CONACAFE found an adequate ground and operated with an agreement of mutual benefit with the private sector. This sector received technical assistance and information for cultivation, in addition to international prices remaining high, exports doubled and the planted surface increased by over 50%.

[6] Azpeitia Gómez, Hugo, *Compañía Exportadora e Importadora Mexicana, S.A. (1949-1958). Conflicto y abasto alimentario*, México, CIESAS-Colección Miguel Othón de Mendizábal, 1994.
[7] García Aguilar, María del Carmen and José Luis Pontigo, "Las reformas económicas del Estados en la cafeticultura nacional", in *El Café en la frontera sur. La producción y productores del Soconusco*, México, Gobierno del Estado de Chiapas, p. 122, cited in Hernández Pérez, Manuel, *Actores sociales, identidades colectivas y participación política en la región cafetalera de Huatusco, Veracruz: 1900-2008*, tesis de doctorado en Historia y Estudios Regionales, Universidad Veracruzana, 2010.
[8] Nolasco, Margarita, *Café y sociedad en México, México*, Centro de Ecodesarrollo, 1985, p. 177; Bartra Vergés, Armando *et al.*, *La hora del café. Dos siglos a mucha voces*, México, Comisión Nacional para el Conocimiento y Uso de la Biodiversidad, 2011, pp. 178-179, and Hernández Pérez, Manuel, *op. cit.*, p. 109.
[9] Nolasco, Margarita, *op. cit*, p. 178; and Bartra Vergés, Armando, *et al, op. cit.* pp. 182.
[10] Bartra Vergés, Armando, *et al.*, *op. cit.*, p. 182.

In 1955 international prices dropped, this provoked a decline in exports and a decrease in revenue for producers and processors as well as for exporters, which caused and internal split in the UNAC and the separation of exporters, who founded the Mexican Association of Coffee Exporters (AMEC). In the UNAC large producers and processors remained, without including smallholder coffee farmers.

The Mexican government participated in international meetings that sought to protect producing countries from the drop in prices. In October 1957 an international agreement, which was called "Pact of Mexico", was signed with other producing nations: Brazil, Colombia, El Salvador, Guatemala, Nicaragua and Costa Rica. Its objective was to stabilize the price of coffee regulating exports. Through this agreement, Mexico committed to promote domestic consumption, reduce the areas under cultivation and increase yields in areas favorable to it.

Achieving these goals meant for the government to intervene with greater rigor in the production and processing of the grain and in export permits.

In 1958, small coffee farmers mobilized in an effort to rely less on exporters, and to request a representation that would involve them more in UNAC.

In this context, on December 30, 1958, the Mexican Institute of Coffee (IMC) was created, a government body that, together with the Ministry of Finance and Public Credit, would be responsible of coffee export permits and several fiscal matters.

The IMC was established as a decentralized dependency of the Ministry of Agriculture and Livestock with a Board chaired by this Ministry and composed of a representative of the Ministry of Finance, one more from the Ministry of Industry and Trade, a representative of the National Bank of Foreign Trade, one on behalf of the producers or their association, a representative of exporters, and finally, one on behalf of roasters or their association. The Board appointed the Director of the Institute.

In the international context the "Inter-American Coffee Agreement" was signed in 1940 and suspended in 1946. From this last year and until 1961 producing nations signed ten agreements on the retention of export crops, but with poor results. In 1962 the formation of the International Coffee Organization Café (ICO) grouped 26 exporting nations, including Mexico, and 13 consuming nations.

The ICO signed multilateral agreements[11] in 1962, 1968, 1976, 1983, 1994, 2001 and the current one agreed upon on September 28 2007, which formally came into force on February 2, 2011.[12]

In México, in the late 1960s, the IMC had regulatory and representation functions before international coffee forums and was responsible for promoting technological developments, and encouraging productivity among direct producers, thus it addressed actions of financing as well as internal and external commercializing of Mexican coffee.[13] It also performed marginal mediation efforts between the three sectors responsible for the production and commercialization of coffee: farmers of small plots, producers and processors of medium and large coffee plantations, as well as exporters. In 1969, the National Register of Producers, carried out by the IMC, reported 92,716 coffee growers, of which 49,234 were smallholders and 43,482 (47%) ejidatarios. In Chiapas, Veracruz and Oaxaca were concentrated 74% of the country's coffee growers.[14]

Since 1973, the Mexican Institute of Coffee (INMECAFE)[15] ceased to be marginal and took an active participation through a public policy for the coffee development in the country, with a reactivated structure that corresponded to the functions to be performed (research, planning, cultivation encouragement, financing of small producers with less than 20 hectares, storage, internal and external commercialization, operation of storage and industrial facilities and management of federal resources channeled to the sector.)

[11] The first and second international agreement of coffee were negociated under the presidency of two Mexicans, namely, Miguel Ángel Cordera Pastor y Fausto Cantú Peña.
[12] Consulted on the ICO website: http://www.ico.org/ES/ica2007c.asp.
[13] Martínez Morales, Aurora Cristina. *El proceso cafetalero mexicano, México,* Instituto de Investigaciones Económicas-UNAM, 1996, p. 74.
[14] INMECAFE (1976). *Plan para el desarrollo de la cafeticultura,* México, INMECAFE, p. 6.
[15] Until 1973 the Institute was identified with the initials IMC, from this year on it changed them for the acrostic INMECAFE.

The INMECAFE planned its course of action through six core programs in the producing areas: organization of producers, payment of advances on harvest, purchases, technical assistance, industrialization and social programs.[16]

The most important role, of course, was the regulation of coffee markets managing the historic quota for exports assigned to Mexico by the ITO, regulated in the System of Commercialization in which were represented the government sector as well as the private and social sectors related to the production and export of the grain.[17]

The program of organization of producers promoted the creation of 1,030 Economic Units of Production and Commercialization (UEPC) with 24,093 partners. At the end of the 1970s, approximately 67% of small producers were members of some of these units.[18] The INMECAFE consolidated 3,369 UEPC with more than 160 thousand associated farmers. In addition, it had the ability to influence the market by increasing their reception centers, which reached a figure of 750. With purchases at an established official price, and with financing alternatives less burdensome than those of the intermediaries, the state-owned company stabilized and leveled the production and purchase prices to farmers.

Producer members of UEPC received advances under a joint commitment, in which all of them had to liquidate their individual debts delivering part of the crop; otherwise the unit would not be supported again and none of its members would receive more resources. Thus, the recovery levels remained close to 90% of the support delivered.[19]

The INMECAFE adopted bold intervention schemes in international markets. It performed directly in the stock exchange of sugar, coffee and cacao in New York and in the international market of London, operating from commercial representation offices established expressly in said capitals. Although the economic clauses of the second international coffee agreement had been broken, Mexico, through several agreements with producing countries –among them Brazil, Colombia, El Salvador, Côte d'Ivoire, and with the support of the Organization of Petroleum Exporting Countries (OPEC) to African coffee producing countries–, contributed via the Geneva Group to the management of the offer in the international market. After an analysis of a long period of cyclical frosts in Brazil, a strategy to defend prices and ensure economic independence was designed under the Charter of Economic Rights and Duties of the States approved by the UN in 1974.

In 1976, the national coffee growing was in a process of frank consolidation. The production was around 4 million bags of 60 kg and it was calculated that 400 thousand families depended on this crop.[20] With this momentum, Mexican coffee cultivation achieved great growth. In 1970, 320,589 hectares were harvested and by 1980 they had reached 418,637, that is, a growth of 36% of the area cultivated with coffee trees in ten years. The increase continued the following decade, for the 1989-1990 cycle there were already 560,415 hectares (34% more), while the volume of production grew 26% and the volume of exports raised 100%.[21]

The effect in face of the producers –especially those with smaller areas- was of great benefit, years later Zapotec, Mixe and Chontal coffee growers from the lower part of Sierra de Juárez in Oaxaca would acknowledge so:

> With the entry of INMECAFE and Banrural, farmers started to somehow modernize coffee cultivation: introduction of other varieties, improvement of the plantations, depulping, drying at home, etc. Bank loans led to a modification of social relations. Rather than borrowing money from the local cacique, godfather or neighbor, the Bank replaced these relationships. These processes occurred in many places in the mountains of Mexico, where small coffee producers live.[22]

In 1978, the renowned journalist Alan Riding wrote in The New York Times:

[16] Hernández Navarro, Luis, "Cafetaleros: del adelgazamiento estatal a la guerra del mercado", in Julio Moguel *et al.* (comps.), *Autonomía y nuevos sujetos sociales en el desarrollo rural*, México, Siglo XXI/ CEHAM , 1992, cited by Bartra, *et. al, op. cit.*
[17] Martínez Morales, Aurora Cristina, *op. cit.*
[18] Nolasco, Margarita, *op. cit.*, pp. 184-191.
[19] Giovannucci, Daniele and Ricardo Juárez (2006). "Análisis prospectivo de política cafetalera, Proyecto Evaluación Alianza para el Campo", México, SAGARPA-FAO, 2005, p. 30.
[20] INMECAFE, *Informe de labores. Agosto de 1976*, México, INMECAFE, 1976, p. 37.
[21] Bartra, *et. al, op. cit.*, p. 197.
[22] VanderHoff Boersma, Francisco, *Organizar la esperanza. Teología campesina*, México, Centro de Estudios Ecuménicos, 1986, p. 46, cited in Bartra Vergés, Armando, *et. al., op. cit.*

…perhaps the most significant thing is that the Mexican Institute of Coffee, a government agency, has struggled and succeeded in reducing the profit margins of middlemen, who in the past wouldn't let the benefits of price increases reach small coffee growers... Nowadays the Institute buys approximately thirty five per cent of the annual national production, which is four million bags of one hundred pounds each, which has been enough to help approximately seventy thousand farmers and to force middlemen to increase their prices....[23]

Also, in a letter written by Rod Chapman for The Guardian, it was noted that:

This year will be a good year for the members of the *ejido* "Emiliano Zapata" of Ocosingo, Chiapas.
For the first time, the coffee they produce, thanks to the rising price of the grain in the world market, will bring them benefits.
"We are using the money to buy new hats, machetes and some colleagues will buy shoes –said Santiago Lorenzo Rodríguez–. And this money will help us feed the family. Yes, you can say that for the first time in years I notice changes in my town and we are making some progress."
Like most of the other farmers of the ejido, Santiago is a Tzetzal Indian, who wears typical traditional clothing. The only thing that he has adopted from the modern world is a pair of black shoes.
Santiago is treasurer of the Economic Unit of Production and Commercialization (UEPC), created by INMECAFE two years ago to organize these farmers' coffee production. Like most of the other twenty members of the UEPC, he reaps about two hundred kilos a year.
…recently there has been an increase in the number of small coffee producers, and as coffee has become a very attractive product for its high price, farmers have turned much of their land into coffee cultivation. Now Santiago receives ten times what he received five years ago.

Even in 1994, the National Coordinator of Coffee Organizations (CNOC), describing the growth of the coffee industry activity noted:

…the strong intervention of the state through INMECAFE [whose actions] were key in the expansion

[23] Cited in Bartra Vergés, Armando, *et. al, op cit.* p. 199.

of the coffee areas by providing improved seeds, coffee plants, technical assistance, small loans and fertilizer in account of crop, etc. The coverage of this state owned company was "integral": it organized the producers, it industrialized and commercialized coffee in the national and international market, it regulated the domestic coffee market and it represented the country in the international organizations linked to the sector. Without a doubt, in this period, coffee growers benefited from the subsidies granted and from the guaranteed price.[24]

The decade of 1980 brought the consolidation of an internal structure of the coffee economy with producing sectors well differentiated into groups of interest:

a) Very small producers in organizations such as CNC, CIOAC and regional autonomous associations.
b) Medium landowners in the National Union of Rural Producers integrated to the National Confederation of Rural Landowners.
c) Medium and large producers in the Mexican Confederation of Coffee Producers.
d) Processors and medium and large producers in Processors of Coffee of Mexico (BECAMEX).
e) Medium and large producers and exporters in the Mexican Association of Coffee Exporters (AMEC).
f) Large industrialized producers, in the National Association of the Coffee Industry (The Association).
g) Small and medium roasters in the National Chamber of the Manufacturing Industry.[25]

And although in the early 1980s INMECAFE captured 44% of the national coffee production, by the end of the decade (1988-1989) its purchasing power reduced to 9.6%. Since 1982, amid economic stagnation and the high inflation suffered by the country, Mexico gradually reduced its participation in the coffee market. Direct purchases also decreased, as well as the level of operation of the coffee processing plant it was in charge of, so did the credits and the transfer of supplies and services to producers.

In 1989 the International Coffee Agreement was broken and in Mexico the influence of INMECAFE was understood by the private sector as a strong monopolistic competition, contrary to the free trade purposes that would be sealed upon signing the North American Free Trade Agreement (NAFTA). After thirty years of being constituted, the institution began a process of transferring its assets to the social coffee sector, which would be operated by the National Indigenous Institute (INI).[26]

Since 1987, business and government sectors were in favor of transforming the functions of the Institute, which led to the government's announcement that INMECAFE was withdrawing from the activities of financing, storage, processing and commercialization of coffee, then laying out that after 1991: "The participation of the Institute will be limited only to the functions of organization, international representation and selected technical assistance",[27] most of its functions would be executed by the SARH (Ministry of Agriculture and Water resources), while commercialization and financing would be assumed by the private sector.

In November 1988 the Coffee Trust (FIDECAFE) was constituted "at the request of coffee producers… and as a prelude of the dismantling of INMECAFE". This fund was negotiated with the federal government and for the 1989-90 cycle it forecasted the granting of credits for supply and commercialization.[28]

Foreseeing the demise of INMECAFE, on April 4, 1990, the government of Oaxaca created the State Council of Coffee of Oaxaca, while the state of Puebla would do the same to create the Coffee Council of Puebla. Both councils anticipated the institutional changes that would distance from coffee growing at national level.

On May 27, 1993, was issued the Decree that abrogated the law that created INMECAFE, which ceased its functions

[24] Coordinadora Nacional de Organizaciones Cafetaleras. Documentos del Primer Congreso de la CNOC, mecanografiado, Oaxaca, 1994, cited in Bartra Vergés, Armando, et. al, op cit, p. 197.
[25] Martínez Morales, Aurora Cristina, op. cit., p. 82.
[26] Giovannucci, Daniele and Ricardo Juárez Cruz op. cit., p. 30.
[27] Bartra Vergés, Armando, et. al, op. cit., p. 205.
[28] Villafuerte Solís, Daniel and García Aguilar, María del Carmen, "Actuación del Estado en la cafeticultura y sus efectos en Chiapas después de la bancarrota de 1989", in Privatización en el mundo rural: Las historias de un desencuentro, México, UAM-Xochimilco, 1998, p. 260

on June 1st. Four weeks after, the Mexican Coffee Council (CMC) was created. This council was formed as a civil association linked to the federal government through the representation of the latter in its Board, in addition to having state and regional councils in the producing entities.

The CMC board of directors was composed by the heads, or the representatives, of the Ministry of Agriculture, Livestock and Social Development (formerly SARH); Finance and Public Credit; and Trade and Industry Development; the governments of the states of Oaxaca, Veracruz, Chiapas, Puebla and Nayarit; the National Bank of Rural Credit, the National Bank of Foreign Trade, FIRA-Bank of Mexico; the CNC; the Permanent Agrarian Congress; the Mexican Confederation of Coffee Producers; the Mexican Association of Coffee Exporters; Section 20 of Coffee Roasters and Millers of the National Chamber of the Manufacturing Industry and the National Confederation of Coffee Organizations.

This Board of Directors appointed the executive chairman, who served as director of the Mexican Coffee Council.

The general objectives of CMC were:

- To design policies to promote and boost productivity in the coffee sector.
- To promote technological modernization.
- To promote […] strategic alliances between productive agents [...].
- To achieve an appropriate placement of Mexican coffee in the international market.
- To represent the interests of Mexico in international forums.
- To ensure that government actions towards the sector, carried out by several agencies, are brought about in a coordinated manner.[29]

This Council did not intervene in the market through direct purchases, due to the economic policy of the federal government and because it had completed the control mechanism of the international coffee offer. Therefore, the coffee policy reduced its action on the processes of production, processing and export.

Between 1994 and 1995, within the subprogram of Support to Coffee Growers by the National Indigenous Institute, the CMC marginally supported some operational processes and coordinated actions with members of the production chain, in order to submit proposals of production equipment and basic infrastructure before the Solidarity Committees that, incidentally, were the replacement of UEPC. Extension services, research, technology transfer, among others, disappeared leaving an institutional vacuum.[30]

In the federal government of 1994-2000, through the program Rural Alliance, the CMC implemented the Program to Promote Coffee Production, providing support to the sector in coordination with the state and regional councils. The Program began in 1996, when the international prices were in full rise up to 300 dollars per hundredweight.

In this context, the federal deputy Agapito Hernández Oaxaca (former agricultural technician of INMECAFE), presented on November 18, 1999, a bill to create the Mexican Coffee Institute; this did not succeed, despite his explanatory memorandum and conscientious structure. At least, in the overlapping paths of digital networking a copy of this proposal can be found (http://www.cafesdemexico.com/images/stories/otros/iniciativa_de_ley_99.pdf).[31]

The state and regional councils of coffee were established as agencies decentralized from state governments for the attention of grain producers, through different services or the direct operation of support programs to the sector.

Each of the 12 coffee-producing states had its own council, with the main function of channeling government funds and implementing policies and programs for coffee producers, as well as gathering information about the sector.

The state councils have great significance in the development of programs, although between them there is a difference regarding their areas of competence, in addition that

[29] Martínez Morales, Aurora Cristina, *et al.*, pp 87-88.

[30] Giovannucci and Juárez Cruz, Análisis prospectivo de política cafetalera, México, Sagarpa, 2006.

[31] The harvest of 1999-200 produced the exceptional amount of 6.2 million bags, however it was preceded by an average of 4.7 million bags during the decade of 1990, with an average of 80% destined to the export and followed by a drop in 2005 of 4 million bags of production, with an estimated of 2 million bags for export (Giovannucci y Juárez Cruz, *op. cit.*, p. 14).

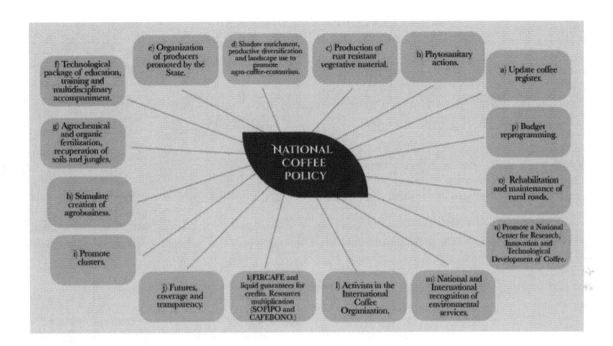

several of them have regional councils that perform the same functions but oriented to coffee micro regions of their entity.

Since 1994, the issuance of Certificates of Origin for the export of the grain was in charge of the Mexican Coffee Council or the State Councils of Coffee.[32]

The Program to Promote Coffee Production (IPC) was applied until 2001, year in which one of its five components, denominated "Development of Instruments to Support the Coffee Policy", channeled resources to develop the National Coffee Register that from 2002 would serve as a support platform.[33]

These years, prices fell. The policy of the 2000-2006 federal public administration was given through direct support to the producers as compensation in periods of low prices that are recoverable in periods of high prices, through a Stabilization Fund of Coffee Prices, besides the productive base was strengthened through transfers to support cultural practices

and the capitalization of land via the Program of Productive Development and Improvement of the Quality of Coffee of Mexico.

In October 2001, when one of the worst crises in the Index of Prices and Quotations happened, the undersecretary of rural Development of SAGARPA summoned the representatives of the production chain to the National Coffee Congress, in which it was agreed that the CMC would be the technical agent responsible for the management of instruments and programs of the sector, and it would also be the conciliation body between economic and social agents linked to farming; it was also agreed that from then on all the programs that granted support would do so directly with the producer, without the intermediary of organizations.[34]

On November 6, 2003, during the First Ordinary Period of the First Year of the LIX Legislation of the Chamber of Deputies was proposed the creation of a Special Commission of Coffee, "in charge of assisting and monitoring, in the field of competence of the Federal Legislative Power, the projects

---

[32] Diario Oficial de la Federación, 26 de octubre de 1994.
[33] Summary of the section "Formación de la política cafetalera moderna", of Giovannucci, Daniele and Ricardo Juárez Cruz, *op. cit.*, pp. 34-40.
[34] *Ibidem.*

and programs to strengthen this product"; on February 2015, this commission submitted its fourth report of activities.

On December 15, 2004, the National Committee of the System-Product Coffee (CNSP) was installed, as a prelude to the dissolution of the Mexican Coffee Council. On September 4, 2005, the members of the Mexican Coffee Council agreed to transform this Council into the Council of Development, Promotion and Defense of Mexican Coffee, A.C., integrated to the System-Product Coffee, "with the objective of renewing and unifying the impulse to the Mexican coffee sector and redirect it towards a real and lasting social and economic development. "

The Mexican Association of the Coffee Production Chain, A. C., hereinafter named the Association, created on May 11, 2006, as well as the state councils of coffee, are both responsible for issuing certificates of origin for the export of the Mexican grain.[35]

Currently, the SAGARPA studies the possibility of a new institutional framework for the cafeticultura and returns to the rectory of the sector, with important national and international presence in organizations such as the International Organization of Coffee (ICO), where two Vice-Chairs are occupied and is a member of three important committees of the same.

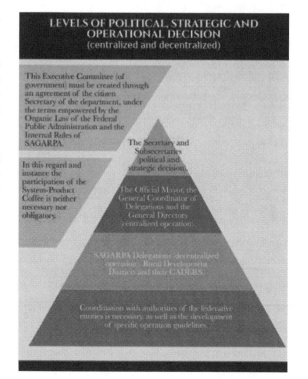

LEVELS OF POLITICAL, STRATEGIC AND OPERATIONAL DECISION
(centralized and decentralized)

This Executive Committee (of government) must be created through an agreement of the citizen Secretary of the department, under the terms empowered by the Organic Law of the Federal Public Administration and the Internal Rules of SAGARPA.

In this regard and instance the participation of the System-Product Coffee is neither necessary nor obligatory.

The Secretary and Subsecretaries (political and strategic decision).

The Official Mayor, the General Coordinator of Delegations and the General Directors (centralized operation).

SAGARPA Delegations (decentralized operation), Rural Development Districts and their CADERS.

Coordination with authorities of the federative entities is necessary, as well as the development of specific operation guidelines.

---

[35] Agreements published in *Diario Oficial de la Federación* from February 7, 2007, June 30, 2007 and August 4, 2011.

PRECEDENTS OF THE COFFEE WORLD ECONOMY

PRECEDENTS OF THE COFFEE WORLD ECONOMY

Great human works have been set in motion with a cup of coffee. Perhaps this is why it is the most important agricultural product in international trade.[1] Not without its ups and downs for many natural, cultural, social and political factors, its trade remains strong and provides employment to millions of people worldwide. In the coffee year 2013/2014, according to the International Coffee Organization (ICO) estimates, exporting countries produced 141 million 60 kg bags. To approach a dimension of this activity, let's recover the value calculated by this organization in 2008/2009 that, with a production of 97 million bags, generated 13.5 billion dollars in foreign currency for the producing countries. The distribution, roasting, grinding and sale of the product and by-products generated further revenue in producing and consuming countries.

Between the 15th and 16th centuries, Yemeni controlled and jealously guarded the production and distribution. Arabs and Turks were the first to fall in love with the drink and to benefit from its trade. Unfortunately for them, a new lover tried to stand in the way of this relationship and, so to speak, snatched their precious object. During the 16th century, Europeans, succumbing to the wonders of this dark brew, made several attempts –that resulted to be vain- to adapt the plants from where they were extracted. Discovering the potential of adaptation in their Asian and African colonies by the 17th century, and later in the American colonies in the 18th century, they globally encouraged the romance with coffee. In the end, the trade had to be shared and subjected to new rules.

The development of the world's leading producer began in the early 19th century. In 1830 Brazil amassed 25% of the production, 30 years later 50% and by the end of that century 75%.[2]

Currently, Brazil keeps its supremacy as producer. The second is Vietnam, although only in 1987 it occupied the 31st position among producers. This change was propelled by the countries that signed the Warsaw Pact and later by the World Bank. The incentive of cultivating the Robusta variety was due to its high content of soluble solids, with a growing market in the industry of instant.

Nowadays the ten largest producers contribute with 86% of the world supply; after Brazil (32%) and Vietnam (19%), are Colombia (9%), Indonesia (6%), Ethiopia (5%), India (4%), Honduras (4%), Mexico (3%), Peru (2%) and Guatemala (2%).[3]

Position	Country	Bags (in thousands)	%
	TABLE 1. TOP 10 GREEN COFFEE PRODUCERS (2014-2015)		
1	Brazil	45,342	32
2	Vietnam	27,500	19
3	Colombia	12,500	9
4	Indonesia	9,000	6
5	Ethiopia	6,625	5
6	India	5,517	4
7	Honduras	5,400	4
8	México	3,900	3
9	Peru	3,400	2
10	Guatemala	3,500	2
	Others (43 countries)	19,166	44
	World	141,850	100

Source: International Coffee Organization.

---

[1] Pérez Pérez, Juan Ramón, *El café, bebida que conquistó al mundo*, México, Universidad Autónoma de Chapingo, 2000
[2] *Ibidem.*
[3] Data for the cycle 2014/2015 from ICO.

There are 70 producing countries, 55 of which are exporters (99% of the production) and therefore accredited members of the International Coffee Organization.

The largest importers in the world are the United States and the European Union, although the former has decreased its purchases, since 30% of the acquisition made in 1990 obtained 24% in 2013. In the European Union, Germany stands out as importer (19%), it has increased its purchases and also became the largest re-exporter of processed product (with a figure that would put it in the third place as a producer).

The list of the ten largest importers is completed as follows: Italy (8%), Japan (7%), France (6%), Belgium (5%), Spain (5%), United Kingdom (4%), Netherlands (3%) and Canada (4%).[4]

These ten countries bought over 84% of the imports made in 2013 and other 24 countries acquired the rest.

Much of the world coffee production is done in small plantations, most of which are family farms, with areas of around 10 hectares and some even smaller, for 70% are 5-hectare units.[5] One hundred and twenty five million people live off its cultivation and production, since harvesting is done manual due to deterrent of mechanization.[6] In Mexico smallholding is more accentuated.

The big problem for producing countries is the price and its variations, whose volatility in sharp declines does not cover the production cost made by farmers and, when there are increases, those who are generally benefited are large corporations that control the market, as well as speculators.

The price of coffee is determined by supply and demand. Firsthand sale is the first link in the commercial exchange. Producers, according to their technological infrastructure, make this first operation with ripe cherry, parchment coffee, wet-process parchment coffee[7] or green coffee. Green coffee beans are the naked beans before roasting and the type used to set prices in foreign trade. Exports are made in 60kg bags that correspond to 132,276 pounds. Green coffee is not a homogenous product; each batch has particular characteristics determined by the type of crop, planting, harvesting, grain selection and processing. For commercial purposes, a classification that takes into account criteria such as altitude and/or region, botanical variety, preparation, grain size, number of defects and grain density is used. It is worth to add the criterion on roast appearance and cup quality, evaluated by tasters and used to set the price of specialty coffees.

The international classification of Mexican coffee is Mexico Prime Washed, whose main characteristics are altitudes between 600 and 900 MASL, on a scale from 400 to 1,400 m. Based on group quality it belongs to Other mild Arabica. The rest are mild Colombian Arabica, Brazilian Arabica and other natural Arabica, and Robusta.

Position	Country	Bags (in thousands)	%	Re-export Bags (in thousands)
1	Estados Unidos	27,016	24	3,248
2	Germany	21,174	19	12,020
3	Italy	8,834	8	3,182
4	Japan	8,381	7	92
5	France	6,713	6	1,014
6	Belgium	5,502	5	4,257
7	Spain	5,137	5	1,636
8	United Kingdom	4,206	4	1,380
9	Canada	4,520	4	1,006
10	Netherlands	3,407	3	1,781
	Others (24 countries)	17,482	16	5,959
	World	112,372	84	35,575

TABLE 2. TOP 10 COFFEE IMPORTERS IN 2013

Source: International Coffee Organization.

[4] Datos para 2013 de la OIC.
[5] *Le marché international du café, de la régulation à la libéralisation, Projet de loi autorisant l'accord international de 2001 sur le café*, citado en "Producción y mercado del café en el mundo y en México", Reporte del CEDRSSA, noviembre de 2014, consultado en Internet, 3 de julio de 2015.
[6] Dato incluido en "Producción y mercado del café en el mundo y en México", *op. cit.*, pero que la OIC especifica como "más de 25 millones de agricultores en pequeña escala y sus familias", boletín informativo de la OIC, consultado en www.ico.org/ica2007.
[7] Esta clase de café se conoce así porque sale de la oreadora a punto de cuerno, conservando aún un porcentaje de humedad entre 16-18% y necesita alrededor de 24 horas de fermentación.

Instability in the price of coffee, in the first place, is due to the variation of unforeseen phenomena, such as drought, frost or diseases. Other influencing factors are market expectations, speculative operations, and fluctuations in exchange rates, among others. High prices encourage production growth, while low prices reduce it. However, the equation is not so simple nor is there a formula to dissolve uncertainty.

A measure to reduce the risks is futures markets. The first commercial export operation is the signature of a standard contract. There are contracts for the sale of physical coffee, that is, one that is stored and ready for shipment. The agreement resulting from the contract establishes a price to which the cost of transportation is added. There are daily transactions resulting from contract of physical products, but also others that are signed committing to a future purchase. The establishment of a future price avoids the uncertainty in the market, which generates a differential between the price of the daily trading and the future one. The differential may increase or decrease; this is called spread risk. When the date of delivery in a futures contract approaches, the futures price and the spot price often converge. Futures prices do not really reflect the physical market and this is where the speculative game comes into play. The delivery of a product can be promised by a certain date, although few futures contracts end in a delivery, and are usually paid off in compensation sales.

The stock market does not set the price. Its basic functions are rather the discovery of prices (agreed upon between the importer and the supplier), risk transfer of prices, dissemination of prices, price quality and arbitration.

The main futures markets are the Arabica Contract of New York, known as contract "C" or NYKC, that covers mild Arabica coffee and allows the delivery of coffee from 19 producing countries, Mexico among them, arbitrated by The New York Board of Trade, merged since 2007 with Intercontinental Exchange (ICE); and the London Robusta Contract, which following the removal in 1982 of exchange controls in the United Kingdom was set up with the London International Financial Futures and Options Exchange (LIFFE). Other futures markets are Brazil and Singapore, joined in 2011 by two stock exchanges in Vietnam.

The futures market has e-commerce as a platform. Through Internet coffee is offered to be delivered after being stored, classified and certified in the proper category. The importing agent also closes the contract electronically. However, the physical market still lacks an electronic format. Roasters seeking green coffee do not buy it blindly, in fact they ask for some samples before purchasing it. The actual delivery of green coffee is made through the document system (physical paper), which can take up to 17 days between the load of coffee, the delivery of documents to the bills of lading, the processing of said documents and the receipt of payment by the shipper. There are proposals to switch to electronic documentation, which would allow this process to be reduced to four days. It is up to coffee traders to accept the use of paperless systems. For now, the solution is partial. The futures market is completely electronic, but only since 2008.

Through the Internet, however, the interest in auctions for the sale of specialty coffees has increased. The first was held in Brazil in 1999. Nowadays it is known as the Cup of Excellence (COE) program, property of the Alliance for Coffee Excellence. The lots offered are very small, but they generate a lot of publicity.[8]

Producing countries have made several efforts to improve the revenues of exported coffee, for lack of a better instrument, they have joined the International Coffee Agreement which they have signed, in its various versions (international coffee agreements of 1962, 1968, 1976, 1983, 1994 and 2001), within the International Coffee Organization, until the most recent, agreed on September 28, 2007, but effective from February 2nd 2011.[9]

---

[8] Para ampliar la información sobre los precios internacionales del café, se puede consultar la *Guía del Exportador de Café*, tercera edición, Ginebra, Centro de Comercio Internacional, 2011, disponible en internet (http://www.intracen.org/guia-del-exportador-de-cafe-tercera-edicion/) y de la cual se extrajeron los datos para redactar una sucinta explicación sobre este tema.
[9] *Boletín informativo de la OIC, op. cit.*

TABLE 3. PRICES PAID TO PRODUCING COUNTRIES IN EXPORTING COUNTRIES

Cents of dollar/pound

Calendar year	2004	2005	2006	2007	2008	2009	2010	2011	2012	2013
Colombian milds										
Colombia	60.83	89.22	89.81	100.05	114.22	138.96	180.55	239.68	166.69	113.91
Kenya	71.01									
Tanzania	26.37	43.69	42.77	59.78	63.38					
Otros suaves										
Bolivia									225.64	203.97
Burundi	27.36	42.93	63.45	80.35	86.19	85.68	85.69			
Cameroon				80.19	79.13	66.05				82.87
Costa Rica	64.87	83.43	89.22	98.64	106.17	106.88	139.86	180.22	173.68	
Cuba	70.18	70.71	70.71	47.14	70.71	70.71	70.71	47.14	70.71	163.04
Dominican Republic	75.70	87.92	86.29	87.13	101.45	106.04	139.43	191.07	147.81	140.98
Ecuador	51.39	91.62	92.45	110.52	143.01	147.09	161.08	227.21	183.90	122.21
El Salvador	39.30	67.10	67.49	75.24	86.05	79.19	109.88	186.74	120.12	95.28
Guatemala	66.91	92.36	91.19	98.31	111.03	109.61	114.77	212.41	165.98	127.66
Honduras	50.23	78.69	80.82	81.63	90.56	83.72	125.16	200.18	145.28	109.57
India	38.32	96.53	95.86	108.03	121.70	136.89	151.08	228.46	161.98	117.06
Jamaica	185.42	244.69	354.89	343.06	348.48	295.97	286.82	302.69	301.44	
Madagascar	46.82	50.80								
Malawi	51.68	83.71	84.58	80.36	76.23	91.31	96.35			
Mexico	90.78	139.03	85.50	90.91	106.05					
Nicaragua	40.87	52.88	58.66	64.30	71.02	71.02	78.54	91.03	60.84	39.52
Papua New Guinea	41.10	62.26	71.28	76.69	111.78	72.75	94.89	141.21	98.82	
Peru	42.43	69.47								
Rwanda	29.46	46.25								
Uganda	37.24	57.86	55.34	65.01	73.32	60.54	87.23	147.03	91.70	70.03
Zambia	64.44	87.18	100.18	106.45	126.70	116.54	129.15	83.79		
Brazilian natural										
Angola									57.05	57.64
Brazil	56.33	87.09	87.02	98.30	109.26	100.80	134.00	224.26	152.29	102.14
Ethiopia	48.85	64.23	58.32	69.83	71.71	77.06	85.36	145.46	102.79	75.98
Indonesia	80.62	117.04	107.52	117.99						
Philippines	66.23	80.00	61.51	81.37	95.52				262.01	
Thailand										203.44
Vietnam									84.42	
Robustas										
Angola	9.92	10.42	12.98	36.05	42.32	40.14	44.59	48.29	47.51	31.37
Brazil	34.83	46.47	62.03	78.94	91.58	73.42	74.22	105.29	104.40	85.29
Cameroon				55.13	52.54	37.74				66.43
Central African Republic	20.17			43.34	45.69	43.59	51.40	72.72	68.73	
Congo, Dem. Rep. of										
Côte d'Ivoire	14.77	11.23	27.99	32.84	51.86	57.52	22.49	28.40	46.29	56.94
Ecuador	29.73	30.96	33.73	64.90	79.26	77.99	80.55	95.26	95.12	78.40
Gabon										
India	30.80	52.42	61.35	79.38	98.12	73.13	77.96	109.60	104.65	94.88
Indonesia	24.17	34.21	52.47	55.80						
Madagascar	19.74	39.24	41.71	69.57						
Papua New Guinea	22.16	24.30	32.89	23.91	34.90	27.57	29.45	37.68	37.24	
Philippines	31.89	41.09	55.52	74.48	88.33	69.38	65.37	100.38	96.38	90.37
Sierra Leone								18.83	51.87	
Tanzania	7.35	14.27	21.45	21.38	35.32					
Thailand	12.83	18.32	46.35	64.67	83.75	90.48	84.50	107.64	103.09	103.77
Togo	21.91	27.92	44.72	56.72	76.94	44.71	42.36	74.14	68.50	66.36
Uganda	26.37	40.82	47.02	55.88	71.09	49.03	55.61	73.54	71.80	67.71
Vietnam	36.00	35.90	54.50	71.11	89.15	65.52	67.18	98.37	87.97	90.23

Source: International Coffee Organisation.

The precedents of this agreement go back more than a century, and are based on proposals of the main consuming country. In 1886 the New York Coffee Exchange was created, in 1901, in this city, the first Conference on Coffee Production and Consumption was held to sign a "solemn agreement in order to prevent an amount of coffee opposed to the attainment of a stable and paid price [...] from entering the market, fighting speculation, setting the bid on advance [...] legally intervening according to economic science", as pointed by Fausto Cantú Peña, former director of the Mexican Coffee Institute and former president of the International Coffee Council, when taking part on the deliberations previous to the consummation of the North American Free Trade Agreement Mexico-USA-Canada.[10]

In 1940, as noted in the chronology, the Inter-American Coffee Agreement was held in Washington to set for the first time export quotas to the signatory countries and thus balance supply and demand.

Regarding the first two Agreements (1962 and 1968), it is considered they served to ensure a large supply to the importing member countries, at a very low price: "the price of roasted coffee, during 1960-70 amounted to 1.43 dollar cents per cup, while once the income of Latin American countries was computed, these received an average of 0.83 dollar cents per cup (less than a penny). Coffee farmers got much less than that".[11]

A sample of the operation of ICO Agreements is the one approved in London on December 3, 1976, by 62 members of the Organization. In the vision of Gilberto Arango Londoño,[12] this Agreement, effective from 1976 to 1982, established the annual allocation quotas for countries entitled to a basic fee, partly fixed and partly variable. It was based on the amount fixed as global annual fee to which was subtracted the amount (relatively small) assigned to each country without the basic fee. The fixed part was 70% of the net annual fee;

the variable was 30%, which was determined based on each exporting member's verified stocks related to the sum of all the stocks of exporters with basic quotas. No member could receive more than 40% of the variable portion of the fee.[13]

Arango Londoño continues to discuss the mechanisms designed by the Agreement, "like everything related to coffee, they are complex, esoteric, tangled, and much patience is needed to read the agreement and decipher it".[14]

Negotiations made for the Agreement of 1989 were suspended on July 4 of that year; thus, the quota system was suspended, as part of the wave that was invading the world, a switch to the free market was made and the large buyers and roasters made their enormous capacity to determine prices visible. Medium and small companies had to sell to large companies who controlled over 70% of the market in Europe and the United States.

Nowadays producing countries process 25% of the total production, they consume the equivalent to 19% and export the rest only as processed coffee: 6%.[15]

About the current Agreement, effective as of February 2011, the International Coffee Council maintains that

Among the most important innovations it is worth to indicate a new Chapter on the development and financing of coffee development projects and the establishment of a Consultative Forum on Coffee Sector Financing, in response to the need for greater access to information on issues related to financing and risk management in the coffee sector, with particular emphasis on the needs of small and medium scale producers. The range of statistical data will be expanded, which will increase market transparency, and a new Committee of Promotion and Market Development will address activities that will include information, research and capacity creation

[10] Participación del Lic. Fausto Cantú Peña en el Foro Permanente de Información, Opinión y Diálogo sobre el Tratado Trilateral de Libre Comercio (TTLC), en el Senado de la República Mexicana.
[11] Carbot, Alberto, *Fausto Cantú Peña: Café para todos*, México, Grijalbo, 1989, p. 171.
[12] Presidente de la Asociación Nacional de Exportadores de Café de Colombia durante 14 años, además de académico, funcionario de Agricultura y de la Banca gubernamental y otros cargos de elección.
[13] Arango Londoño, Gilberto, *Por los senderos del Café. De la gran bonanza a la peor crisis: 1975-1993*, Ediciones Fondo Cultural Cafetero, Santa Fe de Bogotá, 1994.
[14] *Ibid.*, p. 275.
[15] *Ibid.*, p. 322.

campaigns, and studies related to coffee production and consumption.[16]

Although globally coffee consumption presents a significant increase over the past 35 years (from 1.2 million tons in 1980/81 to 8.9 in 2014/15), countries that traditionally import coffee beans keep their acquisitions stable; what has strengthened the market is the demand for differentiated and high quality coffees , instant coffees and prepared beverages, as well as the consumption in Asian countries and Russia.

However, the low consumption in producing countries is paradoxical, with the exception of Brazil and, recently, Indonesia, for the average rate of consumption per person per year is less than 4kg, if this figure were to be reached in all the producing countries it would remove all surplus and, therefore, the permanent problems of price.[17]

Mexico once occupied the third place in world production of mild coffee, although now its participation ranks between seventh and eighth. Additionally it came to be regarded as an important producer of organic coffee and to focus in other coffees that are known as specialty.

During the last three decades, Mexico has produced an average of 1.5 million tons of cherry coffee annually in 746 thousand hectares, approximately, which are equivalent to 4% of the total sown area of the country. In 2013 cherry coffee occupied 3% of the sown surface and generated 2% of the national agricultural production.[18] From every 250 gr of cherry, an average of 1 hundredweight of green gold is obtained.

According to the Plan of innovation in coffee production in Mexico, issued by SAGARPA on November 2011, including producers, laborers, operators of coffee processing plants, workers of industries, café employees, and participants in the commercialization and their families, around three million Mexicans depend on coffee to some degree.

The states of Chiapas, Veracruz, Puebla and Oaxaca concentrate 94% of the production, 85% of the surface,

TABLE 4. COFFEE INTAKE PER CAPITA (KG PER YEAR)	
Country	Kg
Hong Kong	1.1
Cape Verde	1.2
Cuba	1.2
Mexico	1.3
Croatia	5.1
France	5.4
Greece	5.5
Germany	5.5
Brazil	5.8
Ukraine	5.8
Italy	5.9
Austria	6.1
Bosnian	6.2
Canada	6.5
Belgium	6.8
Switzerland	7.9
Sweden	8.2
Holland	8.4
Denmark	8.7
Iceland	9
Norway	9.9
Filand	12

*Data 2015 SAGARPA estimated at 1.7 per capita consumption of coffee (kg./year).
Source: International Coffee Organization.

[16] OIC, Boletín informativo, *op. cit.*
[17] Arango Londoño, Gilberto, *op. cit.*
[18] Datos del Sistema de Información Agroalimentaria y Pesca (SIAP), incluidos en "Producción y mercado del café en el mundo y en México", *op. cit.*

PRECEDENTS OF THE COFFEE WORLD ECONOMY

and 83% of the producers; the rest is distributed in Hidalgo, San Luis Potosí, Guerrero, Colima, Nayarit, Jalisco, Tabasco and Querétaro, in addition to three entities with a minimum production: State of Mexico, Morelos and Michoacán.

Since the Mexican Institute of Coffee was created in 1957, coffee policy posed three objectives: increase yields, increase domestic consumption, and product diversification. Same as those still being posed "given that there has been little progress in their attainment"[19] (as of 2000).

Academic and government studies agree on pointing out that, from 1962 to 1989, the period of major expansion in the national coffee industry occurred due to the rising prices in the international market, because of the validity of international coffee agreements and as a result of the negotiations to regulate the supply between producing and consuming countries members of the International Coffee Organization.[20]

Location	Sup. Sown (Ha)	Sup. Harvest (Ha)	Production (Ton)	Productiveness (Ton/Ha)	PMR ($/Ton)	Production Value (thousands of mexican pesos)
Chiapas	260,129.43	254,020.78	402,099.78	1.58	5,074.88	2,040,607.85
Colima	2,373.00	2,373.00	2,744.20	1.16	5,462.19	14,989.34
Guerrero	47,209.00	45,507.50	48,921.88	1.08	6,717.56	328,635.79
Hidalgo	25,500.00	24,749.00	35,229.00	1.42	4,136.78	145,734.50
Jalisco	3,624.30	3,564.30	5,399.77	1.52	5,434.74	29,346.37
Michoacán	16	16	60	3.75	5,000.00	300
Morelos	52	52	94.3	1.81	4,047.06	381.64
México	479.04	474.04	427.43	0.9	4,752.23	2,031.24
Nayarit	17,739.03	17,739.03	24,634.91	1.39	6,731.58	165,831.99
Oaxaca	142,117.15	138,422.62	129,781.19	0.94	3,835.43	497,767.15
Puebla	73,201.50	56,145.66	148,900.46	2.65	4,947.34	736,661.79
Querétaro	270	270	135	0.5	8,800.00	1,188.00
San Luis Potosí	17,006.43	16,420.43	13,052.00	0.8	2,273.65	29,675.63
Tabasco	1,040.16	1,040.16	848.68	0.82	7,513.73	6,376.75
Veracruz	146,619.41	138,512.81	353,697.22	2.55	4,507.87	1,594,420.43
	737,376.45	699,307.33	1,166,025.82	1.67	4,797.45	5,593,948.47

TABLE 5. COFFEE CHERRY DOMESTIC PRODUCTION 2014

Source: Data of SIAP.

[19] "Análisis Prospectivo de la Política Cafetalera", *op. cit.*, p. 59.
[20] Pérez Pérez, Juan Ramón y Salvador Díaz Cárdenas, *op. cit.*, y "Plan de innovación en la cafeticultura de México", *op. cit.*

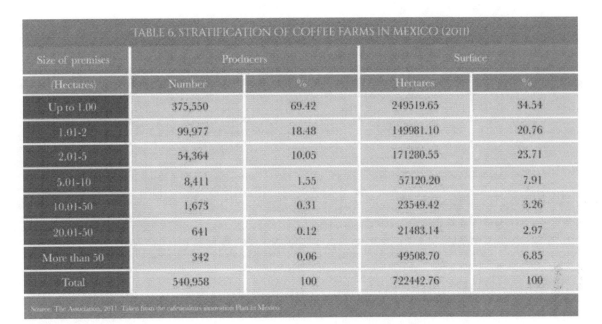

Size of premises	Producers		Surface	
(Hectares)	Number	%	Hectares	%
Up to 1.00	375,550	69.42	249519.65	34.54
1.01-2	99,977	18.48	149981.10	20.76
2.01-5	54,364	10.05	171280.55	23.71
5.01-10	8,411	1.55	57120.20	7.91
10.01-50	1,673	0.31	23549.42	3.26
20.01-50	641	0.12	21483.14	2.97
More than 50	342	0.06	49508.70	6.85
Total	540,958	100	722442.76	100

TABLE 6. STRATIFICATION OF COFFEE FARMS IN MEXICO (2011)

Source: The Association, 2011. Taken from the coffeemakers innovation Plan in Mexico.

The Mexican Institute of Coffee seized this circumstance to organize all the phases of the productive process, including technical assistance and commercialization. From 1973 to 1989 the INMECAFE implemented a program to support the national coffee cultivation organizing producers to improve commercialization procedures, expand the areas cultivated and contribute to overcome the conditions of marginalization in which many of the farmers lived.

Negotiations within the ICO paid off, but they were part of other strategies of the producing countries, these would buy coffee to "futures" in order to sell it on the stock exchange when the manipulations would drop the prices, while they would suspend coffee exports to force a price increase, as described by Fausto Cantú Peña, who participated as general director of the INMECAFE in this strategy.[21]

This was complemented with the removal of "physical" coffee, whose inventories gravitated negatively in the US market, and was sent to Europe. These operations were done jointly by Mexico, Brazil, Colombia and El Salvador to look after the front of the New York Stock Exchange. African countries did the same, with its variants, to look after the London stock exchange.

These measures, according to the referred description, complemented the internal measures of each country; for instance, in Mexico, with higher taxes for exports, market diversification, control and consolidation of export supply, national reserves for domestic consumption and industrialization to sell the processed product. Abroad, another tactic was to get the support of oil-exporting countries to finance temporary retention until the price went up. Strong coffee producing countries bought coffee sold cheap by the weak ones in order to avoid damage to the market and undertake multinational industrialization projects.

This way, the INMECAFE gave to thousand of smallholders, hundreds of large producers and tens of coffee processors, the opportunity to export; however, the federal government

[21] Carbot, Alberto, op. cit.

(as of 1982) opted to take powers from the institute and gradually withdrew the financial resources with which it supported the farmers organization, and facilitated direct sales from producers to the processing plants or directly to the export.

On July 5, 1989, the economic clauses of the International Coffee Agreement were eliminated. The international marketing was open to the free market. In the "Plan for Innovation in coffee production in Mexico,"[22] sponsored by SAGARPA, it is explained that the application "of structural adjustment policies" led the government to the final closure of the INMECAFE in 1993, and from this it followed that "the collection and commercialization have been developed, in part, by autonomous social organizations. The majority, however, has been covered by the old 'coyotes' and transnational companies, that have gone to operate directly in the field where intermediaries used to operate".

In the following years, international prices kept a relative stability that seemed to improve in 1999, when an upturn happened, but whose benefits were not visible, for unilateral

punishments of up to 30 and 40 dollars per 100 pounds of Mexican raw coffee were applied under the pretext of a decrease in quality. From 2004 a price increase began, which allowed the recovery of production costs and a slight upward trend in prices.[23] However, the upturn that happened until 2011, began to decline and since 2004 there was a differential between the world price and the domestic price, which in recent years has increased by up to 30% below the international price.[24]

The commercialization of Mexican coffee is done in the domestic and international market; this one receives more than 60% of the production.

Mexican exports go mainly to the United States, where 78% of foreign sales are placed, a figure that has remained stable but that puts Mexico as the 5th or 6th provider, when for many years during the 20th century it was the first or second. Domestic consumption is among the lowest, for it ranks in the 69th place in the world, with a consumption of 1.2 kg per person per year, in a comparative where the highest consumer is Finland, with 12 kg per capita, and in the case

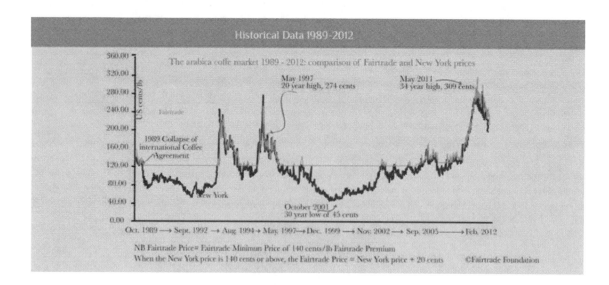

[22] Document issued under the sponsorship of SAGARPA, the Coordinadora Nacional de las Fundaciones Produce (COFUPRO), Universidad Autónoma Chapingo, the System-Product National Coffee, AMECAFE and INCA-RURAL, p. 76.
[23] "Plan for Innovation in coffee production in Mexico", *op. cit.*
[24] "Production and coffee market in the world and Mexico", *op. cit.*

of a producing country, Brazil, with a consumption of 5.8 kg per capita per year.

According to the Prospective Analysis of coffee policy[25], which would serve as a reference for the 2006-2012 federal administration, the increasing globalization and concentration of transnational companies in the coffee industry facilitate their growing influence in supply and demand; hence six trends emerged:

1. Global growth in demand, driven by unconventional markets; although growth in traditional importing countries is slow, in emerging countries like China, Russia, India and Korea it expands rapidly.
2. Decreasing price trend, due to technological innovations but as well because "in Mexico the payment of a daily wage in coffee cultivation is 4 to 7 dollars, in Vietnam it is 1.5 dollars.[26]
3. The biggest opportunities are found in specializations, the largest commercial potential is specialization and differentiation.

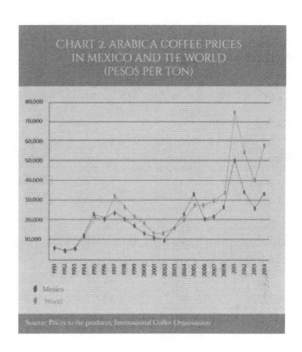

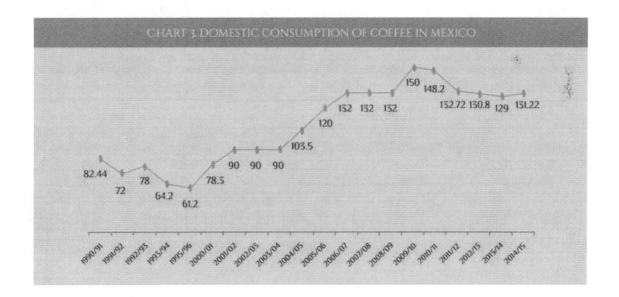

[25] FAO-SAGARPA, *Proyecto Evaluación para el Campo* 2005. *Análisis prospectivo de la política cafetalera,* elaborated by Daniel Giovannucci and Ricardo Juárez Cruz, México, FAO-SAGARPA, 2006 pp. 12-13.
[26] *Ibidem,* p. 44.

País	Producción	Consumo	Porcentaje
Brasil	48,095	19,130	39.78
Vietnam	18,500	1,583	8.55
Colombia	9,200	1,400	15.22
Indonesia	8,500	3,333	39.21
Etiopía	7,450	3,383	45.41
México	4,400	2,354	53.5

CUADRO 7. PRODUCCIÓN Y CONSUMO EN CINCO PAÍSES. CICLO 2010

Fuente: OIC.

4. New phytosanitary standards, a growing demand for coffee that ensures safety (organic, traceable, *food safety*).
5. New social and environmental standards, competitive differentiation and prerequisite for the participation in certain sectors.
6. Decrease of the share of primary production in the value chain, the portion of the retail price of coffee paid to the producer will decline as the added value in the commercialization links of the chain increases.

The cited analysis of FAO-SAGARPA established in 2006 that these trends were already present in the market, and Mexico had the option (without neglecting the traditional production) of exploiting those that placed it as a renowned producer of differentiated coffees (described in 3, 4 and 5).

Ten years ago more than 60 thousand hectares of organic coffee in the country were reported.[27] Nowadays Mexico is considered as the second country that produces organic coffee, second only to Peru: "in two decades [1990-2010], the surface destined to organic production went from 50 thousand to 400 thousand hectares and the sales of such products generate 400 million dollars a year. Organic coffee represents 50% of organic products nationwide".[28]

Without a doubt, our country has a head start as far as coffee production goes. According to the Prospective Analysis of coffee policy, Mexican producers were pioneers in the export of certified organic coffee over 50 years ago; they managed to become the largest exporter of organic coffee for several years and a leader in fair trade; they developed the first instance of a national code for sustainable production and they intensified efforts in the production without fertilizers.[29]

This same study noted that Mexico has the experience and agro-ecological conditions for producing quality coffee. Of the surface cultivated with coffee 35% is located above an altitude of 900 MASL, where high-grown coffee and strictly high-grown coffee are produced; 44% is at a height between 600 and 900 MASL. Regarding growing conditions, almost 99% is made under diversified shade, which gives the crop a great environmental importance because it helps conserve biodiversity and it offers environmental services to the planet, as carbon capture, conservation and recharge of groundwater, biodiversity and natural landscape conservation. Thus, Mexican coffee can engage in highly specialized markets.[30]

[27] Master Plan of the system-product coffee in Mexico, *op cit.*
[28] www.economia.com.mx/10_sectores_donde_mexico_manda.htm, SAGARPA, September 2010.
[29] FAO-SAGARPA, *op cit.*, p. 60.
[30] *Ibidem*, p. 66.

With these possibilities, Mexican coffee can be welcomed in coffee shops, shops dedicated to selling a fine selection and quality that have multiplied in several consuming countries, with preparations that receive bonuses of up to 50% over the price of regular coffee *regular coffee.*[31]

---

[31] Arango Londoño, *op. cit.*

Destiny

Photography:
Martin Barrios

ECONOMY AND INDUSTRY

ECONOMY AND INDUSTRY

Coffee is produced in 15 entities of the Mexican Republic, although only three states (Chiapas, Veracruz and Oaxaca) concentrate more than 75% of the producers, cultivated surface and production volumes. There are 960 municipalities with coffee activity, but of these, only 236 are important, due to the scale of their production.[1]

From a base of 486,194 producers registered by the System-Product Coffee in 2006,[2] 84.2% of them have 2 hectares or less and own 47.2% of the surface. Only 416 producers, that is, 0.08%, have more than 50 hectares and 8.2% own the land. The average surface per unit of coffee production, according to the latest Agricultural and Livestock Census of INEGI,[3] is 1.94 hectares. These data allow corroborating that the crop production belongs mainly to smallholders.

Coffee production occurs in three forms of property: land for common use and two private forms (*ejido* production units and communal production.)

[1] Robles Berlanga, Héctor Manuel, *Los productores de café en México, Problemática y ejercicio del presupuesto*, Subsidios al Campo, México, 2013.
[2] The year 2006 is the date date with more recent data to estimate the land possession percentage of this crop. To May 2014, SAGARPA estimated the participation of 511,669 producers that used 697,366 hectares.
[3] The VIII Agricultural and Livestock Census of INEGI, presented in 2007, is the last census presented to the date.

Indigenous people have great participation in coffee production. According to the VIII Agricultural and Livestock Census, 350 thousand production units have 56.6% of speakers of indigenous languages, with about 30 ethnic groups involved. This population owns 43.9% of the area with coffee and harvests 40.3% of the production volume.[4]

In the 2010-2011 coffee cycle, based on the type of producers with firsthand sales operations for coffee, it was registered that 74.09% were men and 25.91% women. As for the type of firsthand sales by type of coffee in the same cycle, 46.63% corresponded to parchment coffee, 43.61% to ripe cherry, 7.60% to wet-process parchment coffee and 2.17% to green coffee. These data suggest the need to integrate the value chain, extended in the number of producers but reduced in subsequent processes. According to data of the Comprehensive Plan for the Promotion of Coffee of Mexico, 2012, seven marketers in the country concentrate 72% of the purchase activity and wet and dry processing, while most of the roasting process of the national production is carried out in foreign countries, as the 79% of the coffee export is green coffee, 0.6% roasted coffee and just over 20% instant coffee.

In Mexico, 60% of coffee is sold in supermarkets and department stores, around 20% in grocery stores, 6% in convenience stores and 14% in cafés, coffee bars, restaurants and others.

Internationally, it is estimated that coffee has a market value of over 80 billion dollars, while the domestic market has a commercial value of 20 billion pesos. ◖

[4]Robles Héctor and Concheiro Luciano, Entre las fábulas y la realidad, los ejidos y comunidades con población indígena. México, CDI-UAM-Xochimilco, 2004.

PRODUCTIVITY AND COMPETITIVENESS

The humid and sub-humid tropical zones of Mexico are prodigious and generous. The Soconusco and north central regions, as well as the slopes of the Gulf and the Pacific, possess ideal land for coffee cultivation. Harnessing its wealth is a task that requires dedication, but above all, conviction.

Establishing an equitable remuneration for agents of the production chain is imperative. In many crops with extension of less than 5 hectares, producers assume the work of laborers and sometimes do not even reach the equivalent to the minimum salary as payment for their work, due to low prices of the product, determined by international quotations.

In 2014, SAGARPA launches the Coffee National Policy, which seeks, among other things, to increase productivity in Mexico through innovation and technological development.

Within this Coffee Nacional Policy it starts the program PROCAFE the productive impulse the coffee, whose main objective is the renovation and re-population of the Mexican coffee, among other activities.

In this sense, SAGARPA has proposed[1] to promote the funding of the sector and manage risk coverage, in addition to stimulating the creation of agro-businesses to encourage cooperation and ensure coffee purchases in a framework of legality, transparency and equity for the producers. These actions are aimed at profitability and, therefore, at ensuring a level of welfare for the people involved in this stage.

To guarantee an increase in the production, the National Financial of Agricultural, Rural Forestry and Fisheries Development (FND) and the Ministry of Finance and Public Credit (SHCP) structured the Financing Program for Coffee Plantation Renewal launched by SAGARPA, who addresses specific needs of the sector, such as the support to the production of nursery plants, the renewal of approximately 470 thousand hectares of coffee plantations in the five main producing states, the training and specialized technical assistance and an eight year financing scheme. In addition

to this, an increase in the production of quality coffee has been promoted, in order to obtain a competitive product and improve the income of the producers.

With PROCAFE, an activity that is promoting SAGARPA is nurseries with important innovations such as the installation of 32 entched nurseries for the production of 15 million preferentially tolerable to rust, located in the main producing entities aromatic plants annually.

The fragmentation of crops can be taken advantage of by establishing cooperatives that encourage teamwork for a common purpose: to reconstitute coffee growing. It depends on the initiative of the producers to join forces, eradicate individualism and distrust, along with an effective governmental management that provides them financial and technical tools.

Among campaigns of technical assistance, SAGARPA established a process of technological innovation in 56 coffee regions, combining 3,293 Modules of Technological Innovation (MIT) in plots of cooperating producers. Technologies practiced in these modules are low cost and high impact, and the issues attended by technical advisors are, in order of importance, as follows:

1. Production of coffee plant in family
   and community nurseries..23.7 %
2. Fertility improvement in coffee farms 17.3%
3. Pest and disease management 17.0%
4. Productive networks management 9.9%
5. Renewal of coffee farms 9.3%
6. Other (7) 22.8%

In 2015 SAGARPA instituted the network of technical support PROCAFÉ with 400 advisers, whose professional skills would allow it this year to tend to 80 thousand coffee producers in 13 coffee producing entities. Its equipment consists of a field backpack with a laptop and 20 measuring instruments, in addition to other tools to carry out demonstrations on the outline of plantations, to diagnose fertility, plagues and diseases or to level equipment for wet processing of coffee, among other activities.

[1] The measures and actions taken by the Ministry of Agriculture, Livestock, Rural Development, Fisheries and Food presented in this article were expressed by engineer Fernando De La Parra Zepeda, representative of the general director of Productivity and Technological Development of this ministry, during his intervention in the International Coffee Convention, celebrated from July 3 to 5, 2015 in Mexico City.

Competitiveness aims to get consumer satisfaction. Satisfied clients ensure the profitability of a business. Along with the National Committee of the System-Product Coffee and the Alliance for Coffee Excellence, SAGARPA carried out the competition Cup of Excellence Mexico 2015. The event brought together 204 producers of seven coffee growing states. As a result, 20 producers were winners, 18 with scores between 85 and 89 and two of them achieved 90 points, being credited with the Presidential Award. These crops represent the best productions of specialty coffees, which will be auctioned to national and international buyers, reaching a value of up to 50 dollars per pound (the average is 1.5 dollars per pound). The panel of judges was integrated by renowned tasters form United States, Australia, Japan, Lithuania, Poland, Nicaragua, the Czech Republic, and Mexico.

Product differentiation is key to overcome the international price barrier or the even lower price in the domestic market. However, there are producers who do not classify crops by grain quality and lack industrial processes to reach better prices. Accordingly, training is indispensable. Among other actions, SAGARPA established the model on indigenous coffee producing areas to promote the orderly development of production and productivity. Currently, the work is being done in 30 indigenous municipalities of six entities (Chiapas, Oaxaca, Guerrero, Veracruz, Hidalgo and San Luis Potosí). Through a mix of resources from the National Commission for the Development of Indigenous Peoples and SAGARPA, an investment is applied in the coffee production in indigenous zones for the commercialization of differentiated, organic and specialty coffees. The activities carried out in

2015 include the organization of 60 work groups in highly marginalized indigenous communities, the establishment of 60 seedbeds and nurseries for the production of 50 thousand Arabica coffee plants, the delivery of 6 thousand technology packages and technical support with 30 trained and equipped advisors.

In addition, strengthening the infrastructure for processing and roasting is promoted in order to improve competitiveness in the national, international and local markets, coupled with actions to increase coffee consumption in Mexico, whose special emphasis is to strengthen the price of the aromatic in the field and for the national consumer to appreciate the excellence of our coffee, with the perspective as well of expanding them.

Sustainability is a concept whose understanding and relevance is growing to redirect the way in which societies relate and how humans interact with nature. Consumers have become more interested in the economical, social and environmental aspects of coffee production. Producers, not only in response to this demand, but because of the profitability of their company and the preservation of the environment, have to seek new ways of to carry out their processes.

Coffee zones make possible areas with forest cover in the north and southeast of the country, preventing environmental degradation and promoting the preservation of various species, mainly birds, butterflies, amphibians, epiphytes, insects, among others. Maintaining and increasing coffee plantations also helps preserving native species and introducing several shade trees, which allows to catch water in areas surrounding important regions for the conservation of the country's biodiversity.

The proliferation of birds in coffee regions such as the Biosphere Reserve El Triunfo, in Chiapas, even generated a new strategy of certification in the production of coffee, denominated "Bird friendly".[2] A single hectare of coffee under diversified shade contains between 40 and 140 species

[2] Anta Fonseca, Salvador, "El café de sombra: un ejemplo de pago de servicios ambientales para proteger la biodiversidad", Mexico, National Institute of Ecology.

of useful plants, both for familiar and local use as for sale in national and international markets.[3]

Growing areas are valuable lands for farmers and a space of the home we all inhabit. Safekeeping them and providing them the necessary care to maintain healthy crops is a demand to obtain high quality standards. Beyond looking after ejidos, medium or large extensions, their owners have a responsibility we must encourage: the conservation of nature. In a context of troubling climatic variability due, among others, to the overexploitation of natural resources, pollution derived from productive or industrial processes, use of fossil fuels in different phases and in the transportation of goods, and accumulation of non-biodegradable residues, coffee production can be a sustainable business model.

The road is not unknown. Polyculture and shade techniques diversify the utility of the land not only to the benefit of men, but also to the procreation of species of flora and fauna. Welfare extends through social economy with needs and common approaches, aimed at promoting an organizational culture, established by cooperative principles and a practice based on a participative functioning, with a direct and indirect government exercise that facilitates organizational flexibility. This business organization is founded on partnership. The government has had a leading role encouraging this type of structure, and it will give it even more force promoting training and providing relevant information, as well as implementing and operating technical, economical, social and political support programs. This will ensure social sustainability, as women and men, who inhabit the slopes of the Gulf and the central and south Pacific of the country, heirs to a culture instituted more than two hundred years ago, will not have to migrate in search of subsistence options. The enthusiasm and dedication of these people must be channeled to boost the economy of the country. Also, you can add new business organizations. Some of the states of the Pacific slope with low production (Jalisco, Nayarit and Colima), as well as Hidalgo, could increase it. The fate of coffee production is promising. It depends on all to channel it, invigorating good proposals, recognizing their scope and executing them, following them up to their fulfillment and preserving their sense of priority.

[3] Moguel, P. y V. M. Toledo, "Conservar produciendo, café orgánico y cardines productivos", in *Biodiversitas*, México, CONABIO, 2004.

SEEDBED OF PRODUCERS

SEEDBED OF PRODUCERS

Recreational science is an educational resource that consists on the use of games, toys and play experiences as a methodology in the teaching-learning process in order to motivate students to improve their argumentative scientific competencies. Engineer José Joaquín Arriaga, founding member of the Mexican Society of Natural History, resident ofw the Humboldt Society and honorary member of the Society of Geography and Statistics, directed a collection that appeared in Mexico in the 1870s, named Recreational Science, a publication for children and the working classes. In Volume I, Agriculture and Industry, he collected seven legends related to products derived from these subjects and devoted the first to the "Story of a Coffee bean."

In this section, signed by engineer Arriaga himself, is transcribed "the simple and true account that mi friend Mauricio Z has lately sent me by mail…". The person, whose last name is not revealed, tells that in Alameda Central in Mexico City he met a girl who shyly approached him and with shame begged him for money. After exchanging a few words, Mauricio accepts the girl's invitation to visit her house. Upon arrival the scene is distressing and difficult for Mauricio to describe, this man feels sorry for the situation of that family and offers them his help, which little by little increases in favors until the father gets a job as "master carpenter and foreman in the works of the railway from Mexico to Veracruz". And this is how after some time, the family moves to the outskirts of Cordoba, where they get a field of medium extension.

Invited by Manuel, the head of the family, Mauricio agrees to visit them in the Gulf region, where in addition to seeing the girl, her brother and Magdalena, mother of both, looking so much better than the time he met them in the city, he is introduced to Martín, a young man adopted by the family as their own and who helped them to develop their coffee plantation, of which they await their first harvest.
Mauricio is generous narrating the lush vegetation of the tropical environment and step-by-step, between the seasonality of his visit and the event succession, he describes the nature of the bush, its plantation, care needed, harvesting, selection, processing, and roasting. The explanation is accompanied by the dialogue he establishes with Martín, in addition to his own knowledge, heard during the tour of the farm with the young man and Manuel, the adoptive father. This scientific explanation is preceded by a detailed account of the history of coffee in the world, its origin, legends and coffee route, as well as an annotation of the places where it is cultivated in Mexico.

This correspondence that does not take more than thirty pages of a pocket edition, even presents the chemical composition

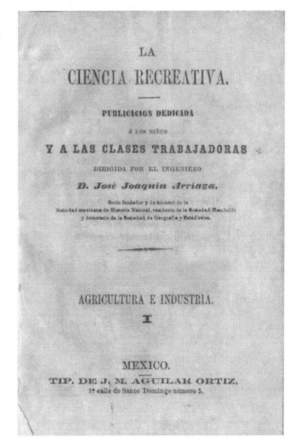

of coffee that was known by that time, which, fortunately, Mauricio says, he had written and kept in his wallet.

The narrative ability to weave an episode in the life of Manuel with the academic explanation impresses by its capacity to synthesize and its attraction power to continue reading in a sort of textbook and scientific literature jewel.

More than a century later, in the mid 1980s, the Coffee Information Center of London, then located across the street from the International Coffee Organization, on 21 Berners Street, published a manual for teachers, whose purpose was to provide a resource to include coffee as "subject, project or as concept of example within the curriculum of regular primary and secondary schools and within food science." Its justification was based on the fact that "coffee plays a vital role in international trade and being a major source of income for many developing countries, it is considered to have a legitimate right to be part of the curriculum".

The outline of this proposal contrasts with that of the engineer Arriaga regarding the formality of its presentation. The outstanding inclusion of historical data, botanic, industrial, commercial, economic and institutional information, is combined with a thorough delineation to expose this knowledge in accordance with the complexity that each grade level deserves, up to college.

The original version of this manual was written in English under the title: "A Coffee Handbook for Home Economics and Catering Students". The Center that developed it later became the Coffee Science Information Centre, a valuable information tool used, for instance, by guides such as Coffee Exporter, edited by the International Trade Center.

Renowned Mexicans who participated within the International Coffee Organization influenced the creation of the Information Center of London. Its experience was irradiated in our country towards the end of the 20th century and reappeared in the year 2000, when the Mexican Academy of Coffee, based in Coyoacán, Distrito Federal, convened, in collaboration with the Postgraduate College, to the "Scientific and technological Meeting for human development of

Mexican coffee cultivation," whose main objectives were to evaluate the state of scientific research and its technological application, in addition to formulate educational plans in this area. One of the presentations given by the Academy encouraged, precisely, the project of a comprehensive School of coffee, as a dynamic concept so that through the educational system a culture of coffee would be generated and the cultures associated to tropical ecosystems would be taken advantage of. This presentation resonated and was later accepted by the municipal presidency of Chocamán, Veracruz, and looked after by the Autonomous University of Chapingo, through the East Regional University Center (CRUO), that since 2009 gives "experiential educational courses in coffee production, for kids, children and grandchildren of coffee producers aged 8 to 14 years." These courses take advantage of the summer holiday to communicate the history of coffee, its primary production (propagation, crop management and harvesting), coffee transformation (wet processing, dry processing and roasting), quality, tasting, and drink preparation (barista), coffee commercialization, differentiated coffees (organic coffee, fair trade), organization of producers and environmental services, and productive diversification in coffee regions.[1]

The main motivation to carry out this experience is related to social impact, 3 million people in Mexico are directly or indirectly linked to the coffee economy, however, migration is a constant in the productive regions and one of the causes is the low level of education, which is intended to be alleviated by forming new generations of producers.

If we are allowed to retake the style of don José Joaquín Arriaga, we could suggest that the activities in this course are developed as follows:

On a Saturday, about to finish school, Antonio went with his grandfather to the town square. Under the shade of a palm tree, don Melquiades asked his grandson what he planned to

[1] Summary of the article "Formando las nuevas generaciones de productores de café en Veracruz, México", of doctor Esteban Escamilla Prado, professor and researcher in CRUO-Chapingo (Hautusco, Veracruz).

do on vacation. Antonio has relatives in the city of Puebla, but the truth is he'd rather stay in Chocamán. Wherever he turns, in the horizon, there are some beautiful green hills, and although sometimes it doesn't stop raining, especially in the summer, he likes the smell of wet earth.

– I don't know –he answers after looking into the sky that begins to be covered by clouds.

Around the square, a car passes by announcing through a speaker some summer courses for children; the grandfather removes his hat and scratches his grey hair.

–I had forgotten to tell you. There is a summer course that you might like. They dropped by the house to tell us they are for our children and grandchildren, so you can learn about coffee, they will also make excursions. Do you want

to go?

– Sounds good.

Don Melquiades enrolled his grandson in the course. "Take good care of him, he said, he's a bit naughty and restless, he'll ask you waaaaaay too many questions."

Every early on July 31, Antonio arrived to the processing plant of the Society of Social Solidarity Catuai Amarillo, which is in the same municipality where he lives, in Chocamán, Veracruz. There were some men talking and talking, the kids were put in front so they would hear the inauguration of the course. Next to Antonio was a girl his age with a pink sweater with buttons and she wouldn't stop fanning herself with her hand.

– If you're so hot, why don't you take it off? –Antonio asked her.

– You're right –the girl took her sweater off and extended her hand– I'm Lupita.

– I'm Antonio.

Shortly after, they were sitting and a girl arrived and explained them what he course was all about. Antonio raised his hand several times to ask many things and Lupita went along.

– And where are we going for a walk?

– Ah, you like walks, don't you?

– Actually I do.

– Well, we are going to a nursery and you will see how vermicompost is made, and the varieties of coffee we have in this processing plant and we're going to Córdoba to visit the Postgraduate College and a farm in Huatusco and the Chapingo University…

– How nice – Lupita said to Antonio while clapping with excitement.

– Yes, it's gonna be great. Hey, Lupita, how old are you?

– Eleven, and you?

– Twelve, I'll be going to junior high school soon.

– And you think you're a big shot?

– A little bit.

The next activity was very entertaining. They told them how coffee was discovered and everything that had to happen for coffee to arrive to America and that it was in Córdoba where

a Spanish gentleman, in a farm with the name Guadalupe, introduced the coffee seeds he brought from Havana, Cuba.

Lupita and Antonio drew everything that was explained to them and they also laughed a lot. The Spanish gentleman was the count of Oñate, Juan Antonio Gómez de Guevara.

Laughter and fun continued, they gave them time for a break, and they played in teams to see who could do the largest line of clothing. Because of Lupita's sweater, the team, where Antonio also was, beat the others.

Then they had the opportunity to meet the rest of the kids, it was time to eat delicious tortas, there were about forty children and they didn't get to meet them all, but there would be other moments in the eleven days that were left.

Before the day came to an end they saw a puppet show and Antonio and Lupita shook hands to say goodbye and agreed to meet very early the following day.

– We'll see if you don't get caught in the covers, Antonio.

The following day they went to the countryside, with notebook and pencil in hand, they noted the explanations of the coffee varieties grown in Veracruz, later, in the classroom, they explained them other varieties grown in the Mexican republic. They also learned how coffee plants grow and both Lupita and Antonio made an effort to make the best drawings of the explanations, but always declared a tie and the teachers gave them VG for very good work.

It was time to learn how coffee is grown. Antonio had some idea because he had seen his grandfather doing it, but he was increasingly more interested on the information he didn't know about coffee. "I have to tell this o my grandfather", he though, "or does he already know?".

– What are you thinking, Antonio? Pay attention to the class.

– Yes, teacher Lupita, he-he.

– Very funny.

The days of the course went by, Lupita and Antonio made more friends but they were still sharing their drawing abilities and reaching a tie. Lupita liked going out and putting into practice what was explained to her in the classroom. They got dirty, they got under the trees that give shade to the coffee plants and they understood that if they could not be all day under the sun neither could a coffee tree.

They went to the nurseries; they kept on playing during the breaks and eating those delicious bean tortas that Lupita's mother prepared. They learned the care a coffee plans needs, how to clean it and prune it, what kind of fertilizers it needs and what is organic coffee. They also learned how to harvest coffee, they talked to them about climate change and how it affects the coffee plant. On the fifth day they went to Huatusco, to the Regional University Center (CRUO), where they met researchers that taught them how coffee is processed. Antonio borrowed glasses from his friend Martín and with a solemn air invited those present to listen to doctor Antonio Gómez. Lupita said to him: "Oh, kid, you still need to study a lot, but you're getting by, soon you'll be in junior high, hee-hee". Antonio only answered: "Very funny."

In the CRUO they also found out about the benefits coffee brings to people's health and Lupita thought that besides being a coffee producer, like her father, she could be a doctor and prescribe coffee to her patients.

The next day, they told the kids how to know the quality of coffee and which parts of the tongue detect the types of flavors, as well as how to tell the properties of coffee by smell or sight. They also got to try some kinds of coffee and some kids liked more soluble coffee and others said organic coffee was tastier.

The following days, Antonio and Lupita discovered that coffee also helps to preserve the environment and that other foods can be planted next to coffee. The day of the partial evaluation arrived. Younger children were nervous and the ones who were older seemed to be more confident, well, this is also like school, Lupita thought, but more fun, Antonio thought.

The day of going to the Postgraduate College (Colpos) in Córdoba arrived, where they went to an area where there were more coffee trees, shrubs the size of adults and larger ones. They also went to the wet processing, where the depulping machines were, after they taught them how coffee is roasted, ground and packaged.

"It smells delicious", was the most heard sentence by all those who were around Antonio.

In Chocamán, the following day, they explained to them how coffee is sold, who determines its prices, and how money moves here and there. Lupita heard with attention the class where they talked about the way in which coffee producers have to organize and she thought that in addition to being a coffee producer, and a doctor, she could be an organizer of the coffee farmers' activities. She would be really busy when she grows up.

Antonio kept on smelling wherever coffee was but he was also very interested in the part where they highlighted the participation of organic coffee in Mexico and the fair trade practices. During this presentation, his arm got tired because he raised it so many times, and his mouth was dry for asking so many questions, but at the end of the day he was very pleased, he had so many things to tell his grandfather.

Almost by the end of the course, they taught them how to make different coffee preparations, how to be baristas, they gave them delicious cappuccinos and Lupita thought that besides being a producer, a doctor, an organizer of coffee farmers, she wanted to be a barista. So many things you can do around coffee.

The last day was the moment for the second and last evaluation. It was also the day when the kids presented to his parents everything they had learned. When Antonio's turn arrived, his presentation was somehow long, but very entertaining, he talked and talked and talked of everything he had seen in the course and as support he used the drawings of Lupita, whom he recognized for her artistic qualities. At the end of the presentation there was a big applause and a little tear that rolled on don Melquiades cheek, while he proudly said to his row mate: "That's my grandson".

SCIENTIFIC RESEARCH AND ACADEMIA, TECHNOLOGY TRANSFER AND INNOVATION

SCIENTIFIC RESEARCH AND ACADEMIA, TECHNOLOGY TRANSFER AND INNOVATION

In Mexico various researches are conducted in order to design and promote sustainable strategies for coffee growing areas. Scientific activities are based on three core concepts: research, training, and technological development. These tasks are performed in different institutions, most of them public and located in the producing states.

The works study almost the whole coffee process. Genetic improvement, in-vitro micropropagation, agrochemical and organic fertilization, shade material, experimental nurseries, phytosanitary measures, agronomic evaluation, physical and organoleptic description of coffee varieties, experimental plots, worm farms, diversification of production in coffee plantations focused on non-timber species and of importance for the conservation of biodiversity, study of species of shade trees and tree diversity in coffee plantations, soil conservation and changes in coffee plantations, cartographic analysis of coffee watersheds, among others.

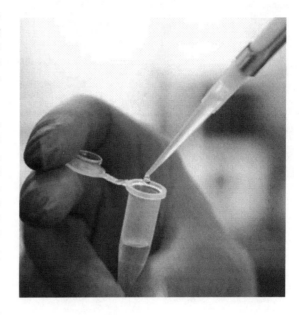

Research regarding the management and control of pests and diseases has special attention. Among the projects that stand out are the efficiency of microbial agents for rust control, coffee rust epidemiology and strategies for its management, genomics and transcriptomics of the infection process of rust, production of specialty coffees in the face of coffee rust epidemic, isolation and evaluation of microparasites as biological control of rust, integrated pest control in coffee plantations, with special approaches to rust and coffee plant root nematodes that cause corky root disease and more.

Facing the problem of climate change, scientists from different disciplines have created research networks to propose comprehensive solutions, among the analyzed topics are the innovation for organic production of coffee, organic participatory certification, shade management in coffee plantations, polyculture, strengthening for the production of organic coffee, social and environmental characterization and diagnostics in coffee watersheds, quantification and valuation of ecosystem services in agroforestry coffee systems, biodiversity conservation through herpetofauna indicator species and in diversified coffee systems, analysis of microclimatic variables that have an impact on agroforestry coffee systems, monitoring systems, database and computing of the coffee system, agro-ecology, climate change and environmental services, legal protection of coffee plantations for their conservation as biodiversity safeguards and biological corridors, maps of coffee plantations and habitat aptitude for priority bird species for the conservation, and many more.

Also, technological innovation projects in the service of coffee production are implemented, for example, for dry processing, the technique on sun drying bed, among other schemes for research, training, and technological development.

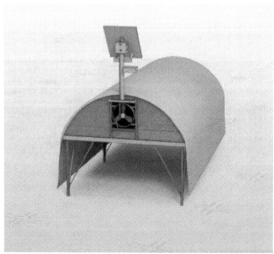

Solar energy drying bed for grains. United Nations Coffee Company UNICO and LABYCEL. Micropropagation of crops.

CENACAFE

CENTRO NACIONAL DE INVESTIGACIÓN, INNOVACIÓN Y DESARROLLO TECNOLÓGICO DEL CAFÉ

Training and counseling needed by the producers to jump-start the value of their product have spread in many. Researchers have also assumed the role of trainers in the facilities of the institutes or through fieldwork. In order to support this prodigious task, SAGARPA create the National Center for Research, Innovation and Technological Development of Coffee (CENACAFE), as the spearhead for technological innovation, technical assistance, applied research and infrastructure for the sector.

Institutions that currently carry out researches about coffee growing in Mexico are the following:

The effort of Alfonso Rochac to elaborate the *Dictionary of Coffee*, edited in 1964 by the extinct Pan-American Coffee Office (New York), will be taken up by SAGARPA with

the development of an encyclopedic dictionary, which will incorporate historical data, technical-agronomic, plant genetic, environmental ethno-ecological, industrial manufacturing, commercial, economic, social, cultural, political-diplomatic and legal terms, etc.; also, it will gather the studies of the International Scientific Coffee Association and other research and higher education institutions that deal with situations relevant to the subject. This will allow a broad, permanent, deep and comprehensive vision of all the categories that affect coffee production, agronomy, industrial technology, marketing, as well as economics, sociology,

ACADEMIC INSTITUTIONS	
CRUO-UACh	East Regional University Center of the Autonomous University of Chapingo
CENIDERCAFE	National Center for Research and Development of Coffee Regions
ECOSUR	El Colegio de la Frontera Sur
INIFAP	National Institute of Forestry, Agricultural and Livestock Research
UASLP	Autonomous University of San Luis Potosí
UAM-I	Universidad Autónoma Metropolitana-Iztapalapa
UV	Universidad Veracruzana
UMICH	Michoacan University of San Nicolás Hidalgo
CIATEJ	Center for Technological Research and Assistance and Design of the State of Jalisco
CIESTAAM	Center for Economic, Social and Technological Research in World Agro-industry and Agriculture
CICADES A.C.	International Center of Coffee Production Training and Sustainable Development
INECOL	Institute of Ecology
CAFECOL	Agroecological Center for Coffee A.C.
COLVER	College of Veracruz
PRONATURA	Pronatura A.C.
ITSZ	Higher Technological Institute of Huatusco
CP	Postgraduate College Campus Córdoba
CINVESTAV	Centro de Investigación y de Estudios Avanzados del Instituto Politécnico Nacional
CICY	Scientific Research Center of Yucatán A.C.
INCA Rural	National Institute for the Development of Rural Sector Cpabilities A.C.
	Institute of Biotechnology of the UNAM
	Institute of Ecology of the UNAM
SMGE	Mexican Society of Geography and Statistics
INECC	National Institute of Ecology and Climate Change

anthropology, biochemistry and medical issues involved in this activity. The whole universe contained in a grain.

This task has been preceded by the "Scientific and Technological Meeting for Human Development of the Mexican Coffee Production" [1] and the First International Coffee Conference. [2] These events are followed by many other conferences, seminars and reunions, where academics of higher education institutions and researchers of national and regional centers have attended, as well as from professional associations and of interest in business, industry, diplomacy, among which the International Coffee Organization stands out.

---

[1] Celebrated in November 2000 convened by the Academy of Coffee and the College of Postgraduates (teaching and research institution in agricultural sciences).
[2] Held in the International Coffee Organization (ICO) from May 17 to 19, 2001 in London.

PERMANENT CONVENTION

PERMANENT CONVENTION

Among other twenty sections, José María Morelos, in his Feelings of the Nation, wrote in Chilpancingo on September 14, 1813:

> 12-. That as the good Law is superior to every man, those dictated by our congress should be such that they oblige constancy, moderate opulence and indigence; and in such a way that the wage of the poor is increased, his customs improved, and ignorance, rapine and theft dispelled.

Two centuries ago, fighters, ideologists, liberal and conservative politicians, were confronted to defend their interests. Finally, the independence from the Spanish empire was consummated on September 28, 1821. A new nation was being erected, not without hesitation and distress, doubtful of its identities and eager persecutor of syncretism.

Coffee has been present during all this time. It is said that priest Hidalgo was fond of chocolate, but we will not know for sure if the meetings promoted by *doña* Josefa Ortiz de Domínguez were also accompanied with coffee. We have tried to recover the relation of Mexicans with the precious rubiaceae. We are not imaginative, although in our minds several unconfirmed facts have remained and we assume that our readers will have much to contribute after inspecting this interactive book and the encyclopedic dictionary of coffee.

We are, however, certain of the potential of this product, of the love bestowed to it by millions of peasants, and of the often-inequitable compensation they have received for their work. So it is no coincidence that we have recovered the feeling of Morelos, who synthesizes a higher aspiration that we have rarely managed to achieve. The pro-independence priest doesn't talk about peasants or coffee production. However, we can bring his words up to date to consummate a fair coffee policy, attached to the law and directed by a congress that encourages constancy and patriotism, moderates opulence and indigence, in such a way that it increases the wages of farmers and improves its customs.

The direction of an economy of this size exceeds a simple desire or good intentions to improve their situation. Social, political, economical and technological conditions are very distant from the concept of Morelos. It's the feelings of the nation that should prevail along with the rationality of this knowledge era. Perseverance and dedication arise from an affinity and conviction to complete a task. It is easy to distinguish coffee promoters; gathering them to gain a common benefit has brought mutual conveniences that couldn't prevail.

The institutional framework in relation to coffee production has to be reconstituted. Women and men are dedicated day by day to magnify a national tradition. Their effort cannot be isolated. It needs to converge at a plenary where their experience is shared and enhanced with the voices of all of those involved in the value chain of coffee cultivation. The problems embedded in this activity, which is generous with nature, the society and its economy, could be solved in a pluralistic and democratic environment.

This call would bring together laborers, producers, processors, roasters, industrials, scientists, moneylenders, traders, marketers, distributors, tasters, baristas, and consumers, as well as other professional services involved, in order to share their vision and channel their purposes. From their field of competence, each of these actors is essential for the stimulation of the coffee industry. The dialogue must transcend the shrub for laborers, the laboratory for scientists, the desk for planners of public policies, warehouses for producers, highways for distributors, halls for tasters, bars for baristas and cafés for consumers.

From July 3 to 5, 2015, in Mexico City, the International Coffee Convention Mexico took place, where people involved in the coffee sector from around the world gathered, convened by the federal government through the Ministry of Agricultural, Livestock, Rural Development, Fisheries and Food. This event presented discussion panels that covered several topics focused on training and strengthening of the sector. Extension and innovation strategies, good agricultural practices, technical support, financing and capitalization for producers, commercial micro-propagation of plants improved by embryogenesis, development of new varieties, production of coffee hybrids, biotechnological rust control, research and innovation networks to attain sustainable coffee production, coffee and climate change, supplier development programs, technical assistance model and technology transfer, marketing and commercial practices, among other topics, were exposed and debated in a cordial and plural environment between scientific experts and farmers with ambition, promoters of

public policies and enthusiastic entrepreneurs, plus a bevy of people from different walks of life but stimulated by the commitment to develop coffee production.

Instituting this convention permanently would allow meeting for the good we all expect. Only through mutual understanding and cooperation we will be able to agree on effective and far-reaching plans that will determine the fate of our community and industry.

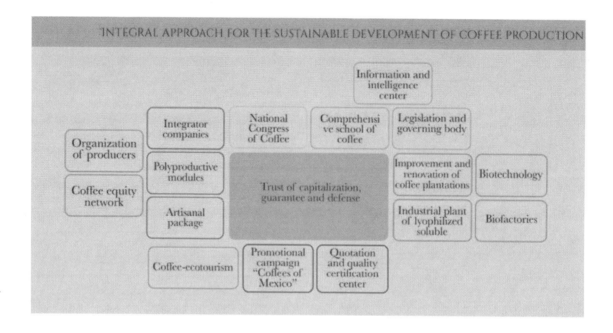

Nature

Photography:
Martín Barrios

THE JEWEL OF MEXICAN TROPIC

THE JEWEL OF MEXICAN TROPIC

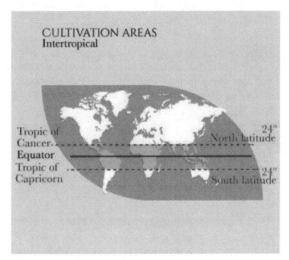

CULTIVATION AREAS
Intertropical

Tropic of Cancer

Equator

Tropic of Capricorn

24° North latitude

24° South latitude

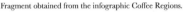

Fragment obtained from the infographic Coffee Regions.

The origin and production of the coffee bush can be found on the extensive strip of land located north and south of the equator, between the tropics of Cancer and Capricorn. The production of coffee is distributed, specifically, in four continents: Africa, America, Asia and Oceania.

The tropic, relative to the tropics: a solar year. It derives from Greek and means to turn, due to the fact that by the time the sun reaches one of the tropics, it seems to return on its own trajectory and to head towards the opposite tropic, an angle defined by rotational and translational axes.

The Tropic of Cancer, the place of the globe where the sun reaches its zenith on the summer solstice day, is the parallel 23° 27′ N latitude. The Tropic of Capricorn, the place of earth for zenith of the winter solstice day, is the parallel of 23° 27′ S latitude. This area was called torrid since the earliest times of knowledge, because it was thought that most of it was not inhabited due to its excessive heat, that is, since the sun would be in its zenith, with its perpendicular rays. However, cool, temperate and healthy countries were found afterward in such area, where there are almost perpetual spring and autumn seasons because nights last almost twelve hours, and the cool wind blows during the day, which pass by several leagues of sea, cooling off the sun rays and therefore causing frequent rainfall. This is why there are, in several parts of this zone, two harvesting seasons per year and trees full of flowers and fruits all year long.

The American hemisphere's inter-tropical zone is located on the Pacific, Nazca, Cocos, South American and Caribbean tectonic plates.

The tropics are astronomical measurements and the inter-tropical zone occupies 40% of the total surface of the planet.

According to an agro-ecological classification, there are three geographical types of tropics: the humid tropics, mainly located on the coastal plains; the sub-humid or dry tropics, and the monsoon tropics of the highlands. There are, nevertheless, enclaves with tropical climate within their boundaries and some others with desert climate.

Mexico has 200 million hectares, out of which only 30

million can be devoted to agriculture. This figure, however, may decrease to 20 million hectares if erosion processes continue.

The hot and humid tropical climate represents 9.6% and the hot and sub-humid tropical climate 15.7% of the national territory, that is, 50 million hectares.

In regard to the agricultural surface, the humid tropical climate consists of 27.5% and the sub-humid one 9.4%, which means approximately 11 million hectares.

The surface devoted to the cattle industry comprises 86 million hectares, out of which the humid tropics represents 7.4%, and the sub-humid ones 9.2%, that is, 14.5 million hectares.

In reference to the 60 million hectares of forest areas, there are 13 million hectares associated to the sub-humid tropics and 8 million more to the humid ones.

Our geographical tropics are defined as a climatic and bio-geographical reality limited by isotherms and isohyets with well-defined minima (an average of 16 to 18° in temperature and precipitations of 800, 1200 and even 2500 millimeters), distinct vegetation in rainforests (tropical moist forests, deciduous and semi-deciduous forests, evergreen forests), forests (even cloud forests), savannas, wetlands and mangroves (mangroves are forests covered by sea tides; they are maritime rainforests located in lagoons and/or coastal saltwater lakes, which are currently contaminated and preyed on as reservoirs for fish farming).

These tropical regions are located in the state of Veracruz –almost all of it–, in the Huasteca region, which is comprised by parts of San Luis Potosí, Tamaulipas and Hidalgo, as well as the Sierra Norte and Sierra Negra of Puebla; the whole states of Tabasco, Campeche and Quintana Roo, and the northern border of Chiapas and Yucatán, with the exception of its northern coast. They also stretch out from the Soconusco region by the Guatemalan border to the southern part of Sinaloa at the latitude of Mazatlán, encompassing the coastal zones and the Sierra Madre Occidental, mountain range located in the states of Guerrero, Michoacán, Jalisco, Nayarit and Colima.

In this regard, cultivating the beautiful shrub that produces the cherry, that is, the coffee bean, was a decisive action for settling and exploiting the tropics on both sides of the country, on the Gulf and on the Pacific.[1]

The climate

Coffee is cultivated by analyzing, in the first place, the climate and by taking into consideration factors such as soil depth and texture, wind regimes, solar lighting, shading and air humidity. The best average temperature for the environment is 25 degrees Celsius, which is within a range of 18 and 30 degrees, without having large variations between daytime and nighttime temperatures throughout the year. It is also possible to grow coffee at lower temperatures, but winter frosts are detrimental.

Coffee requires 1,500 millimeters of rainfall distributed throughout most months of the year (an average demand of at least 120 millimeters per month). A drought lasting more than three months may affect the productivity in some cases. Relative humidity must be in between 70 and 90% during the rainy season, and in between 40 and 50% during the

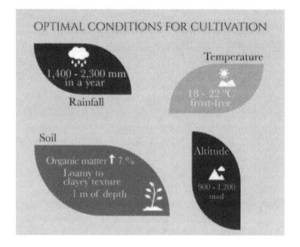

OPTIMAL CONDITIONS FOR CULTIVATION

Rainfall
1,400 - 2,300 mm in a year

Temperature
18 - 22 °C frost-free

Soil
Organic matter ↑ 7 %
Loamy to clayey texture
1 m of depth

Altitude
900 - 1,200 masl

[1] Cantú Peña, Fausto, "Planeación y Aprovechamiento Integral del Trópico Mexicano" (fragment), lecture presented in the Formal Sitting to join in as an active member of the Mexican Society of Geography and Statistic, México, June 2010.

dry season. Solar radiation must range between 1,600 and 2 thousand hours per year, an average of 4.5 to 5.5 hours of sun light per day.

· There shouldn't be any winds with such length and speed that may cause damages to the plantation, like defoliation, premature wilting of the flower or fruit fall, among others.

There are four main environmental factors that have an effect on the quality of coffee:

1) Altitude. Quality classification for washed mild coffee is related to the altitude where it was grown, that is, to the height above mean sea level (AMSL). The varieties cultivated at a higher altitude develop more acidity and aroma, providing better taste and higher value. It grows and fructifies well in plots located between 500 and 1,600 meters AMSL, the most favorable being between 800 and 900 meters. However, altitude is not indispensable for harvesting quality beans, since latitude, temperature conditions, rainfall, relative humidity and the amount of sunshine, all of them, contribute to that goal.

2) Humidity. Due to the fact that coffee is a seasonal crop, it requires a good distribution of rainfall. The activity of the plant decreases during dry periods, which favors the production of floating coffee, generating losses. In order to counteract the effects of droughts, the plantation must be placed adequately, the shades must be employed properly, and good management must be provided to the plantation itself. There are crops that depend on irrigation in countries like Vietnam; this is a positive resource for having better control on the plantation, however, it increases the cost of production.

3) Soil. The land's texture, gradient, depth, pH, organic matter content and fertility are elements related directly to production. In order to have a taproot, the coffee tree requires deep terrain, located in permeable subsoil and rich in topsoil. Optimal soil is dark, has a loamy texture, and is found in low-gradient surfaces (<5%); its particles are balanced between clay, silt and sand, which also determine proper permeability and porousness. The best level of acidity in the soil should be around 5 and 5.5 to improve the nourishment of the plant.

Organic matter must be considered in order to obtain high productivity of the crop, since it helps retain moisture and constitutes an important source of nutrients for the coffee tree.

Soils that derive from volcanic ashes, classified as andisols, have high content of organic matter, high porousness, low apparent density, great water retention capacity and the clay fraction dominated by an amorphous material. All of these properties favor fertility and generate high-quality coffee trees.[2]

4) Presence of frosts. Hoarfrosts have a negative impact. The quantity and quality of the crop normally decrease for those plantations located where there are frosts. They also impair the production of subsequent years by having to renew the plantation. ◖

[2] Ramos-Hernández, Silvia and David Flores-Román, "Comparación de dos fuentes fosfatadas en suelos volcánicos cultivados con café del Soconusco, Chiapas, México", in *Agrociencia*, vol. 42, núm. 4, México, Colegio de Postgraduados, 2008, pp. 391-392.

GEOGRAPHY

The coffee-growing area of Mexico is located approximately between 14° 50' and 22° N latitude, at an elevation between 200 and 1,600 meters above sea level (MASL).

Coffee cultivation in Mexico is found in the mountain ranges located close to the Pacific Ocean and the Gulf of Mexico. The production areas have their own specific conditions and are distributed as follows :[1]

Mexico has a wide variety of plantations due to their elevation above mean sea level (AMSL). There are areas located almost at sea level, such as the plots in Nayarit, but there are also others found at an altitude higher than 1,400 meters. Actually, 21.5% of the crops are located in areas no higher than 600 MASL; 43.5% can be found between 600 and 900 meters, and the remaining 35% are plots located higher than 900 MASL. [2] According to data from

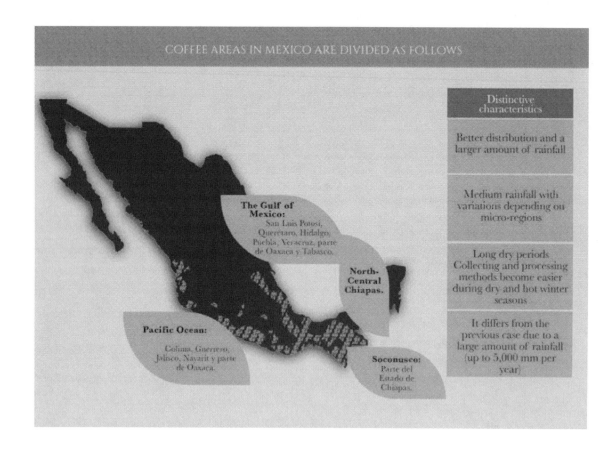

COFFEE AREAS IN MEXICO ARE DIVIDED AS FOLLOWS

The Gulf of Mexico: San Luis Potosí, Querétaro, Hidalgo, Puebla, Veracruz, parte de Oaxaca y Tabasco.

North-Central Chiapas.

Pacific Ocean: Colima, Guerrero, Jalisco, Nayarit y parte de Oaxaca.

Soconusco: Parte del Estado de Chiapas.

Distinctive characteristics

Better distribution and a larger amount of rainfall

Medium rainfall with variations depending on micro-regions

Long dry periods Collecting and processing methods become easier during dry and hot winter seasons

It differs from the previous case due to a large amount of rainfall (up to 5,000 mm per year)

[1] Taken from the Master Plan of the system-product coffee in Mexico. Final version for validation, August 2005, consulted online June 9, 2015.
[2] *Idem.*

the Agricultural Information System (SIAP) of SAGARPA, the total cultivated surface of the country in 2014 was 737,376.45 hectares.

Regions within the states of the Republic

Chiapas

In 1846, Italian Jerónimo Manchinelli brought 1,500 coffee trees from San Pablo de Guatemala; these were planted in his estate, La Chácara, in Tuxtla Chico. Carlos Gris, however, contributed in a more significant way to the crop by planting, during a period of ten years that started in 1871, 100 thousand coffee trees in his estate, Majagual, located in the cacao-growing area of Cacahoatán, in Soconusco. Coffee growers of German nationality settled down in this region and laid the foundations so that the entity would remain the main producer of Mexico. This crop extended eventually from Chiapas to part of Oaxaca.

At present, production is concentrated in 4,620 localities of 88 municipalities. According to data from 2006 provided by the Commission for the Promotion and Development of Coffee from Chiapas, there were 175 757 growers working in 242,689 hectares. The Agricultural Information System considers Chiapas as the main national producer, having

40.3% of the production in 2014, which means 499 105 tons of cherry coffee, almost the total of all the Arabica variety and just a bit of Robusta.

Colima

The *Agriculture, Mining and Industries Bulletin*, published in 1891 by the Ministry of Development, indicates that since 1821 there were coffee shrubs in some smallholdings of Colima City. The same source refers that the state legislative body issued a decree granting several franchises to whomever got involved in the production of this crop; two companies were established, but only one of them succeeded notoriously –the other one

failed–, since the person in charge was knowledgeable about the subject matter. Different information, commonly known, indicates that the crops owned by general Mariano Michelena in Uruapan proliferated to other areas of Michoacán and even to Colima; it is highly probable that this crop was taken to the latter by Mr. Ignacio Ochoa towards the middle of the 19th century.

In the state of Colima, 2,519 hectares of coffee were harvested during the year 2006, which means 1.91% of the total surface with perennial crops, and a total production of 2,530 tons, having an average output of one ton per hectare. The value of harvested coffee production for 2006 was estimated in $7,787,090.00, which represents 0.25% of the total agricultural production value of the state for that same

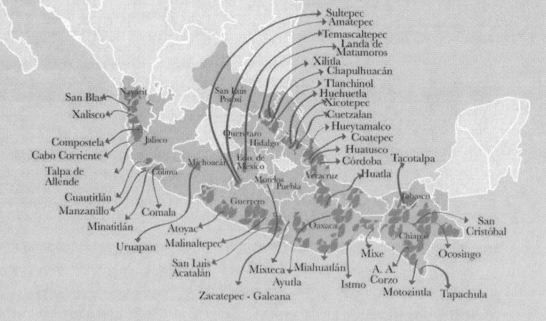

SOME COFFEE REGIONS
The variety of regions and areas where coffee is cultivated in Mexico makes possible a production of differentiated attributes; in addition our quality allows us to compete with the great coffees of the world.

San Blas
Xalisco
Compostela
Cabo Corriente
Talpa de Allende
Guautitlán
Manzanillo
Minatitlán
Uruapan
Comala
Atoyac
Malinaltepec
San Luis Acatalán
Mixteca
Ayutla
Zacatepec - Galeana
Miahuatlán
Istmo
A. A. Corzo
Motozintla
Tapachula
Ocosingo
Mixe
San Cristóbal
Tacotalpa
Huatla
Córdoba
Huatusco
Coatepec
Hueytamalco
Cuetzalan
Xicotepec
Huehuetla
Tlanchinol
Chapulhuacán
Xilitla
Landa de Matamoros
Temascaltepec
Amatepec
Sultepec

Nayarit
San Luis Potosí
Querétaro
Hidalgo
Edo. de México
Jalisco
Colima
Michoacán
Morelos
Puebla
Veracruz
Guerrero
Oaxaca
Chiapas
Tabasco

year. Coffee is cultivated in the municipalities of Comala, Cuauhtémoc, Minatitlán, Villa de Álvarez and Manzanillo. There are 783 growers (Fundación Produce Colima).

Estado de México

The total cultivated surface of coffee in eight municipalities is 474.04 hectares. Amatepec, Sultepec and Temascaltepec stand out due to the amount they produce. In 2014, SIAP registered a production of 427.43 tons of cherry coffee.

Guerrero

The cultivation of coffee started in the Costa Grande region during the last decade of the 19th century. Initially, it was sown by Claudio Blanco in El gambito estate, known today as El porvenir, but it was twelve years later in a different estate, El Estudio, when commercial exploitation of the crop started.

The crop expanded rapidly in the Atoyac mountain range under the control of hacienda owners and landowners until 1940, when the agricultural unit of the coffee-growing zone from Atoyac was handed over to the peasants. At the end of the 1950s, the first wet coffee processing plants of the region were built, some airstrip runways were constructed so that coffee could be taken away by light aircrafts, and new coffee-growing areas were promoted.

The bean is cultivated along the Sierra Madre del Sur, part of the Sierra Mixteca or the range of Zempoaltépetl, which is parallel to the Pacific coast. In 2014, according to data provided by SIAP, the state of Guerrero produced 49 921 tons, ranking as the fifth state in production.

Hidalgo

The state of Hidalgo, in its bordering areas with San Luis Potosí to the north, and Veracruz and Puebla to the east, has favorable conditions for growing coffee; this explains why this crop arrived to such area from Córdoba and Coatepec, Veracruz, at the beginning of the 19th century.

In general terms, the crop in Hidalgo is characterized by its low productivity and a fragmentation of its production into small units, not surpassing an average size of 2 hectares, which dissuades people to become interested in it and to create a favorable environment for its growth and care.

Hidalgo is currently the sixth most important coffee-growing estate of our country, with a surface of 25,000.00 cultivated hectares, which represent 3.5% of the national total, although it has 2.13% when referring to production, that is, according to SIAP.

The crop is produced in 743 localities found in 25 municipalities. Most of the producers are indigenous people (77%), while the rest are considered mestizos.

Jalisco

According to the story of the arrival of coffee to Michoacán, that is, regarding the beans that Mariano Michelena brought from Moka, in the island of Mauritius, and that he started cultivating the plant in Uruapan, Mr. Ignacio Ochoa took the first seeds from there to Colima, where they were sown, and from there the crop proliferated to other parts of the state and to the south of Jalisco.

Based on the National Coffee Register, there were 1,905 growers in Jalisco during the period 2004-2005; they were distributed in 10 municipalities having 3,832.69 hectares devoted to the cultivation of coffee.

According to SIAP, the state produced 0.47 of the national production in 2011, ranking in the ninth position.

Michoacán

In 1824, coming back from Moka, general José Mariano Michelena obtained coffee seeds, which were sown for the first time in the garden he had in his house, in the capital city of Michoacán. Once the plants grew to a specific size, they were planted in the plots of his hacienda La Parota, located in the valley of Urecho; these plants reproduced in an extraordinary manner, to the point they became brushwood that needed to be controlled. Due to the beauty of the trees, people from some communities went there to pick them up

in order to have them as ornaments for gardens and even for smallholdings. Thus, these trees were taken to Tacámbaro, Taretan, Los Reyes and Colima. The crops from the valley of Urecho eventually expanded on to Ario, Tacámbaro, Aguililla and Coalcomán.

In 1876, a selection of coffee from Uruapan won an international prize in the Centennial Exhibition in Philadelphia, due to its quality and good taste. This encouraged several people from Uruapan to devote themselves to the crop. "It rivals with the

one from Moka", wrote Matías Romero. As a consequence, at the end of the 19th and beginning of the 20th century, this coffee was acknowledged as the "best coffee of the world" by artists, scholars and plenty of international travelers, such as José Martí himself.

According to a report from the Agriculture Ministry, developed in 1960, coffee production in Michoacán was scattered in 1 230 hectares of plots devoted to avocado, citrus, and other fruits. Back then, the annual harvest was estimated in 32 086 *arrobas*, which equate to 369 tons.

Currently, the low production of coffee is restricted to the municipalities of Uruapan, Tingambato, Ziracuaretiro, Tancítaro, Tingüindín, Peribán and Tacambaro; its cultivation is complementary to the avocado orchards. Most of the production generated in these places basically concentrates in Uruapan, from where it is distributed through the company called La Lucha.

Morelos

Jaime Salvet started cultivating coffee in Cuernavaca and Yautepec in 1809. That same year, on March 6, he requested the viceroy of New Spain, Pedro de Garibay, to be exempted from paying municipal royalties and tithes on the coffee produced in his haciendas, San Diego de Barreto and

Nuestra Señora del Rosario Xuchimancas, located within the jurisdiction of Cuernavaca, nowadays the state of Morelos. Such request was declined. In May 1810, Salvet had almost 350 thousand coffee plants located in tree nurseries; these plants were about to be planted.

is an important agricultural activity for the entity, devoting 6% of cultivated area, and 29% of perennial crops, that is, according to the Nayarit Coffee Council.

Both Michoacán and Morelos have the merit of being, along with Veracruz, the first places of the country where coffee crops developed. Unlike Veracruz, however, which ranks second in national production, Michoacán and Morelos have the last positions.

According to data provided by SIAP, Morelos produced 94.3 tons of cherry coffee in 2014.

Nayarit

Crops of coffee proliferated in the country in the Pacific and Gulf of Mexico between 1850 and 1890, especially in areas with warm and moist climates, with hills, cliffs and mountains located between 200 and 1500 meters above sea level, where it was complicated to cultivate tobacco, sugar cane, cotton and other commercial crops from the colonial period. Several small and large plantations, therefore, were established in Michoacán, Guerrero, Colima, Nayarit and Jalisco.

The state of Nayarit has three coffee-growing regions: Centro (Tepic and Xalisco), Norte (Acaponeta, Ruiz, San Blas, Santiago Ixcuintla, Del Nayar and Huajicon), and Costa Sur (Bahía de Bandera, Compostela and Santa María del Oro). Even with the low production Nayarit has, when compared nationwide –since it produced 24,634.91 tons of cherry coffee in 2014, according to SIAP–, coffee-growing

Oaxaca

Coffee plants were taken to Oaxaca from the states of Veracruz and Chiapas once their production consolidated. José María Cortés, the parish priest of San Agustín, was the first person to sow a patch of land in Loxicha in 1854. The crop proliferated during the following twenty years without much impetus, since the peasants of the area were more interested in cultivating cochineal. This activity was eventually abandoned due to unemployment caused by the emergence of artificial dyes. This encouraged peasants to cultivate coffee, a more profitable product, especially when its international price increased (a 55% rise in 1888), promoting the interest in coffee even more as well as increasing the number of peasants devoted to such crop. As a consequence, a coffee-growing area was developed in the district of Pochutla, which prompted the creation of the community called Pluma Hidalgo. This town eventually became a great producer of coffee in regard to amount and quality: it got the highest prices in the market at the end of the Porfirian dictatorship.

According to SIAP, Oaxaca contributed with 8.8% of the national production in 2014, ranking fourth among producing states. Based on the National Coffee Register, 101,272 producers devote 138,422.62 hectares to coffee, which are located in 150 municipalities of the state.

Puebla

Just as the cultivation of coffee expanded from Córdoba and Coatepec to other parts of the state of Veracruz, it did to the plantations located in the neighboring state of Puebla, mainly to the Sierra Norte, where there are favorable climate conditions and propitious soils for production.

Coffee is grown by 625 communities in 55 municipalities in Puebla. The extension of land used for this purpose is, according to SIAP, 56,145.66 hectares, divided in 46,745 plots. The cultivation is performed along the rugged mountain range of the Sierra Madre Oriental. This entity ranked third in production (15.2%) in 2014, when it generated 148,900.46 tons of cherry coffee.

Querétaro

The communities of Neblinas and Agua Zarca, located in the municipality of Landa de Matamoros, are part of the coffee-growing area of the Huasteca and the Gulf of Mexico. They are found at an altitude of 900 meters above sea level and within the limits of the Sierra Gorda of Querétaro, where there are special micro-climatic conditions that allow the region to be determined as coffee growing. Cultivation in this area began at the same time as in the Hidalgo and San Luis Potosí Huasteca, in the second half of the 20th century.

Coffee production in Querétaro is only practiced in the municipality of Landa de Matamoros. There are 296 producers cultivating 270 hectares; its production is quite minor, since it almost represents 0.08% of the national total (135 tons of cherry coffee), according to the report given by SIAP for 2014.

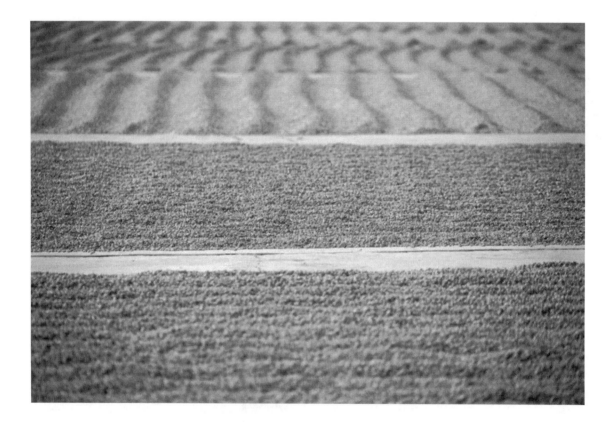

San Luis Potosí

Coffee plantations proliferated in the regions of the Pacific and Gulf of Mexico during the 1850-1890 period. The crops located in the central and northern part of Veracruz expanded to the Sierra Norte of Puebla, and to the Huasteca regions of Hidalgo and San Luis Potosí.

There are 17,379 coffee producers in the state of San Luis Potosí with 26,947 plots in 13,769 hectares devoted to the crop, that is, according to the System-Product Coffee San Luis Potosí, 2007. This crop is limited to the regions of Xilitla and Tamazunchale, where four municipalities contribute with 96% of the production in 305 localities. Based on the information provided by SIAP in regard to 2014, the production of cherry coffee was estimated in 13,052 tons.

Tabasco

The expansion in the cultivation of coffee that took place at the beginning of the 19th century, originally developed in Córdoba, Jalapa, Coatepec and Teocelo in the state of Veracruz, stands out for the impact it had in the Sierra Norte of Puebla and in the Huasteca regions of San Luis Potosí and Hidalgo. It also involved, however, the neighboring state of Tabasco and the median elevations of its territory.

A total of 1,354 producers registered in 2008, having 1,006.1 hectares located in the municipalities of Tacotalpa, Teapa, and Huimanguillo, which are found in between 150 and 60 MASL. This indicates that, among other conditions, coffee from Tabasco originates in low areas. According to SIAP, Tabasco produced 848.68 tons of cherry coffee in 2014.

Veracruz

Although there are records indicating that, on the one hand, Spaniard José Antonio Selebert introduced the first coffee trees in 1784 through the port of Veracruz –so that they could be planted in Córdoba and Coatepec–, and that in 1808, on the other hand, the priest José Santiago Contreras and parish priest Andrés Domínguez sowed in Coatepec and Teocelo some coffee seeds brought from Cuba by Spaniard José Arias, most historians agree that it was Juan Antonio Gómez de Guevara, Count of Oñate, who brought the first coffee beans from Havana in 1812, and started their cultivation in Hacienda de Guadalupe, located in Córdoba.

In 1826, Bernardo Herrera had half a million plants producing coffee beans. In his Hacienda El Mirador, acquired in 1829, Karl Christian Sartorius did some experiments with the product, and, in 1850, he became the first person to employ water for removing the coat of the coffee bean.

The crop of coffee expanded from Veracruz to central and southern parts of the country: Puebla, State of Mexico, San Luis Potosí and Guerrero.

According to SIAP, the state of Veracruz is the second producer of the country, totaling 27.6% of the national production (365,333 tons of coffee cherries in 2014). This state devotes 138,512.81 hectares for the crop, especially for the *Coffea arabica* varieties: *Tipyca, Bourbon, Mundo Novo, Caturra,* and *Garnica.* The coffee-growing area is found in 842 communities and 82 municipalities, where there are 86 thousand producers, covering the regions of Atzalan, Misantla, Coatepec, Córdoba, Los Tuxtlas, Texonapa, Zongolica, Huatusco, Papantla and Chicontepec.

In January 2002, according to the Norma Oficial Mexicana NOM-149-SCFI-2001, this coffee was acknowledged with the designation of origin "Café Veracruz".

FROM GENOMICS TO SUSTAINABLE PLANTING

FROM GENOMICS TO SUSTAINABLE PLANTING

Since the 17th century, when European merchants, physicians and scientists started to typify the coffee shrub and its beans, data provided have multiplied substantially and enabled the understanding and manipulation of this valuable natural product. As a consequence, this has allowed a better use of the resource. At the dawn of the 21st century, the technology employed for scientific observation has reached and perhaps exceeded the dreams of those scholars from the past. New information and communication technologies enable the immediate interaction among the most recognized specialists of the globe. It is due to these advancements that a group of international researchers achieved to sequence the coffee plant genome. This accomplishment was published in the Science journal on September 5, 2014.[1] This contribution sheds light on the evolution of caffeine biosynthesis. Based on the genes of Coffea canephora, better known as the Robusta variety, the researchers involved determined that caffeine followed an independent genetic process, similar to the functions found in tea and chocolate, which also produce it. This means that the coffee tree did not inherited caffeine genes from a common ancestor, but that it developed them by itself.

This discovery allowed scientists to theorize on the chemistry of the plant and to determine the use of caffeine as an insect repellent.

Academic studies also emerge from the observation of a problem and the procurement of its solution. Human impact, through agricultural production, has caused environmental deterioration with serious consequences, which we are still able to repair. Analyzing different cultivation systems and industrialization processes becomes vital to change the course toward coffee-growing sustainability and profitability. ●

Plant technology laboratory in *Cinvestav Irapuato*

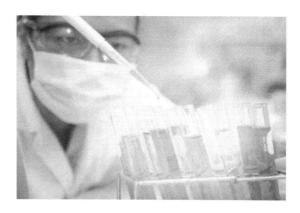

[1] France Denoeud et al., "The coffee genome provides insight into the convergent evolution of caffeine biosynthesis", in *Science*, September 2014 DOI: 10.1126/science.1255274.

COFFEE SPECIES AND VARIETIES

Coffee species and varieties[1]

Genetic resources of a species are represented by the total number of plants such species can interchange genes with in order to improve its characteristics, that is, the possibility of obtaining hybrids through the process of breeding plants. In the case of a coffee tree, these genetic resources include around one hundred species considered part of the genus *Coffea*, and the lesser-known species of the genus *Psilanthus*.

Commercial species are *C. arabica, C. canepora, C. liberica, and C. excelsa.* The Arabica kind produces larger and denser coffee beans. Robusta coffee produces darker brown colored beans, of course, if they are compared to Arabica —which has a green bluish color—. Also, caffeine content distinguishes both species: Robusta holds in between 1.6 to 2.4%, while Arabica ranges from 0.9 to 1.2%.

The difference regarding the beverage produced by each of these species, is that Arabica is mild, with pleasant aroma, acid characteristics and medium body, whereas Robusta produces a bitter and less aromatic beverage, with an inferior level of acidity, but having good body and strong flavor, special aspects for instant coffee.

Globally, there are over 200 varieties of Arabica coffee in the world (*Coffea arabica* L.), without considering the great diversity of wild types found in Africa, its place of origin.

In Mexico there are two commercial species of coffee: *Coffea arabica* L., the most important in extension and dissemination, contributing with 95% of the production, and Coffea canephora Pierre ex Froehner, commonly known as Robusta coffee, manly cultivated in the hot lowlands of the states of Veracruz and Chiapas.

COFFEE GENEALOGY

Kingdom :	Plant
Subkingdom:	Angiosperm
Class:	Dicotiledonea
Sub class:	Simpeleta or Metaclamidea
Order:	Rubiales
Family:	Rubiaceas
Gender:	Coffea
Sub gender:	Eucoffea
Species:	coffea arabica coffea canephora coffea liberica and many more.

[1] Taken from the book *Variedades de café en México*, de Alfredo Zamarripa Colmenero and Esteban Escamilla Prado, edited by CRUO-Chapingo, 2002..

The most important varieties grown in Mexico are described
in the following table:[2]

| VARIETY | ORIGIN | HEIGHT | COLOR | | SENSIBILITY | PRODUCTION/ PLANT (KG) |
			BUDS	FRUITS		
Typica	Ethiopia	High	Tanned	Red	It cannot tolerate direct sunlight nor winds	2.8 to 4.8
Bourbon	Africa	High	Light green	Red or yellow	It tolerates direct sunlight and winds.	5.0 to 5.1
Caturra	Brazil	Low	Light green	Red or yellow	It tolerates direct sunlight	4.9 to 8.9
Mundo Novo	Brazil	High	Dark green	Red	It tolerates a dry period and can recover	5.4 to 16.6
Maragogipe	Brazil	High	Tanned	Red and large	It cannot tolerate direct sunlight	Low
Oro Azteca	Mexico	Low	Dark green	Light red	High productivity, resistant to rust	6.7 a 12.1

[2] Included in the book Manual para la Cafeticultura Mexicana. Cuaderno 1: El Café en México, edited by Instituto Nacional de Capacitación del Sector Agropecuario-Consejo Mexicano del Café, 1996, p. 26.

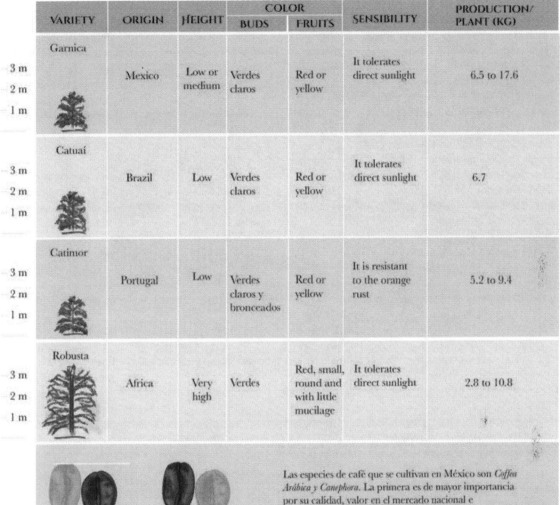

VARIETY	ORIGIN	HEIGHT	COLOR		SENSIBILITY	PRODUCTION/ PLANT (KG)
			BUDS	FRUITS		
Garnica	Mexico	Low or medium	Verdes claros	Red or yellow	It tolerates direct sunlight	6.5 to 17.6
Catuaí	Brazil	Low	Verdes claros	Red or yellow	It tolerates direct sunlight	6.7
Catimor	Portugal	Low	Verdes claros y bronceados	Red or yellow	It is resistant to the orange rust	5.2 to 9.4
Robusta	Africa	Very high	Verdes	Red, small, round and with little mucilage	It tolerates direct sunlight	2.8 to 10.8

Arabica Robusta

Arabica Robusta

Las especies de café que se cultivan en México son *Coffea Arábica y Canephora*. La primera es de mayor importancia por su calidad, valor en el mercado nacional e internacional y por su extensión territorial.

Manual for the Cafeticultura Mexicana. Notebook 1: The Coffee in Mexico edited by the National Institute of Training of the Agricultural Sector Mexican Advice of the Coffee, 1996, p. 26.

It is worth highlighting the Garnica variety. It was bred by advanced generations of selected Mexican Mundo Novo 15 and Yellow Caturra 13. This variety was developed by INMECAFE in Campo Experimental Garnica, in Xalapa, Veracruz, where it got its name. The hybridization process took place in 1960, while the commercial distribution of "pesetilla" in 1978. The Garnica variety consists of 18 short-height selections with great production capacity and exceptional vigor.[3]

In 1995, the National Institute of Forestry, Agriculture and Livestock Research (INIFAP) released the Oro Azteca variety with the intention of reducing the damage caused by coffee rust in Mexico. In this regard, Zamarripa and Escamilla[4] indicate that this variety.

is the result of breeding the Red Caturra variety, which confers low-height and efficient characteristics, with the hybrid Timor, which provides resistance to the fungus Hemileia vastatrix. This interbreeding was carried out by doctor Aníbal J. Betancourt[5] in the International Center of Coffee Rust (CIFC), in Oeiras, Portugal, back in 1959. The selection process and generational advancement started in African and American countries in 1960.

The Agronomic Research Institute of Angola (IIAA) and the Federal University of Viçosa (UFC) in Brazil participated in the early stages of selecting promising materials. In 1981, the National Institute of Forestry, Agriculture and Livestock Research (INIFAP), from Mexico, received and installed advanced progenies of coffee trees in its Campo Experimental Rosario Izapa. These progenies were examined individually in order to know their agronomic qualities. After their characterization, the generational advancement was carried out with the target of homogenizing the different genotypes by selecting 21 progenies, which became the material for the adaptation testing performed in different regions: Soconusco in Chiapas, the coast of Oaxaca, Coatepec, Veracruz and Sierra Norte of Puebla.

The Oro Azteca variety can be considered of low height and semi-compact type, in regard to the Typica form. When the fruit is ripe, it is ellipsoidal in shape and red in color. The percentage of normal *planchuela* type beans (flat berries) was higher than 90%, a similar figure presented by the Red Caturra witness. The percentage of hollow fruits produced varies according to altitude, registering 6%. Peaberries (caracoli) presented lower values than 5%.

The tests of adaptation carried out between the 1986-1987 to the 1994-1995 agricultural cycles in different coffee growing regions indicated that production varied from 32.3 to 55.2 hundredweights of dry parchment coffee per hectare. On average, in 27 evaluated environments (localities per year), the output was 40.1 hundredweights of dry parchment coffee per hectare, exceeding by 37% the output of the improved Red Caturra variety.

[3] INMECAFÉ-Nestlé, *El cultivo del café en México*, Instituto Mexicano del Café, 1990, p. 39.
[4] Zamarripa y Escamilla, *Op. cit.*, pp. 20-21
[5] Zamarripa y Escamilla, *Op. cit.*, pp. 20-21

STRUCTURE OF THE COFFEE TREE[1]

The coffee tree

A coffee tree can live up to half a century. It starts blooming at the age of 3 and its production becomes profitable since it is five years old.

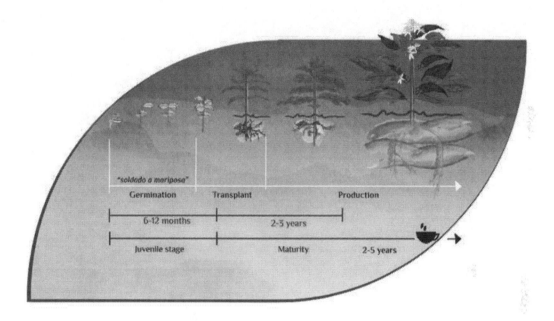

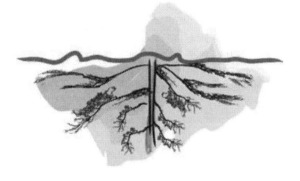

Root: It is the part of the plant located in the soil, from where it gets its nutrients. It consists of a main root and several others considered secondary. The main root, strong, thick and long, penetrates the soil vertically, reaching over a meter in depth. Secondary roots, which are thinner, grow horizontally and inclined; sixty percent of these roots grow within the first 30 centimeters.

[1] Text taken from the book *Manual para la Cafeticultura Mexicana. Cuaderno 1: El Café en México*, edited by Instituto Nacional de Capacitación del Sector Agropecuario-Consejo Mexicano del Café, 1996, pp. 19-21.

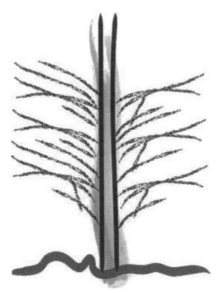

The main stem: It is the part of the plant upholding the branches, leaves, flowers and fruits. It is straight, woody, thin, flexible and well branched from the base. Buds that eventually become main lateral branches can be found on the main stem; serial buds only originate on vertical branches.

Main branches: These are the parts of the tree that grow on the stem of the plant. Leaves, flowers and fruits sprout from them. They are long, flexible, round and well provisioned with leaves and axillary buds. Serial buds generate from two to four inflorescences and each of these has four to five flower buds.

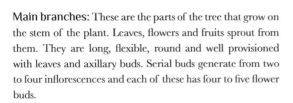

Leaves: These are the organs that help the plant breathe and elaborate its nourishment. They are perennial, simple, opposite, and membranous, with a short stalk, oval shaped and tipped. Their borders are wavy. Their color is dark green and shiny in the upper part, and light green in the lower. The new leaves show a tanned or light green coloring; the definite color develops afterward. The length of the leaves ranges from 10 to 15 centimeters and their width from 4 to 7 centimeters.

Flowers: Flowers contain the reproductive organs of the plant, where the seeds needed for new coffee trees are formed. They are small, white, and quite fragrant and are found in the axillary cavities of the leaves. A complete flower is composed of sepals, petals, stamina and pistils. All of these are found at the tip of a little stem called peduncle (the small end of the flower). There are five sepals and they have a cup-looking form called calyx; the flower is found in this cup and then we have the five petals all merged in one at the base, which surround the reproductive organs. All petals together are called corolla. The reproductive organs are the stamina: they are the filaments with a bulky tip, similar in appearance to a pin. Pollen grains are formed in on such tip, called anther. The pistil can be found surrounded by the stamina.

Coffee flowers look like white small five-petal stars. They remain open only for a few hours since they wilt as soon as fertilization happens. However, a coffee tree blossoms constantly, giving the impression that its flowers last several days. It can render up to 30 thousand flowers in a year. A sweet fragrance exudes from the coffee trees during blooming season.

The time it takes for each fertilized flower to become a completely ripe cherry ranges between six to seven months. The process speeds up when having hot climate, and slows down with low temperatures.

The fruit: The fruit contains the coffee seeds. It is a drupe with smooth and shiny surface, thin pulp and it is easily detachable. It is green when unripe, and red or yellow when it's fully developed, which is why it is called coffee cherry.

Cherry coffee has pulp and parchment. The pulp is composed of the endocarp, which is the skin, and the mesocarp, which is the mucilage (also called honey).

Parchment coffee is composed of endocarp, silverskin and green coffee. The first one is the skin that covers the two seeds; it is known as parchment. The silverskin is the silver-colored layer covering each of the seeds. The two seeds found in the core of the fruit are called green coffee.

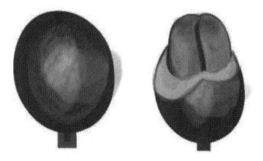

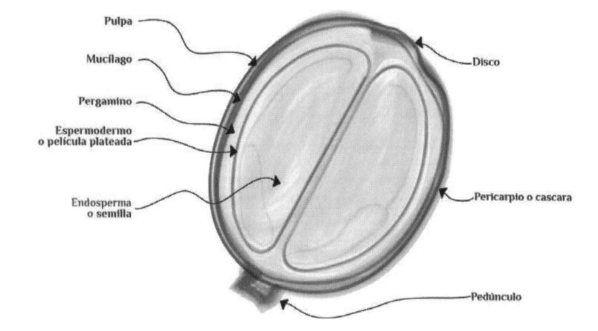

Pulpa

Mucílago

Pergamino

Espermodermo
o película plateada

Endosperma
o semilla

Disco

Pericarpio o cascara

Pedúnculo

Culture

Photography:
Enrique Garza Cantú

THE CROP

THE CROP

Nurseries and reproduction

"… the quality of coffee is generated in the plantation, while the processing and toasting only procure its preservation"[1]

The reproduction of the coffee plant can be done with seeds or by cuts. The most common method is with seeds: it allows to breed different varieties in order to improve the plant. In contrast, a replica of the "parent plant" can be ensured by employing the method of cutting.

The terms seedbed, plant farming or nursery are employed to refer to the places designed to reproduce, induct and manage plants. The reproduction procedure has been going on for several years, as can be confirmed by the experiences collected and shown by Federico Hannemann in a publication from 1928 .[2]

Hannemann suggested to have the seedbed installed at the beginning of the rainy season. He recommended to select "the best possible land, to plow it with a depth of 25 to 30 centimeters, to have the ground clods undone and small furrows made of 8 to 10 centimeters wide by two deep, with a separation of 20 centimeters between each, [so that] the seed could be placed in the furrows with a distance of half a centimeter per seed."

A previous step should have been the preparation of the seed by cutting the fruits from the lush trees, selecting the

[1] Santoyo Cortés, V. Horacio y Salvador Díaz Cárdenas, Esteban Escamilla Prado and J. Domingo Robledo Martínez (1996). *Factores agronómicos y calidad del café*, Programa de Investigación y Desarrollo en Regiones Cafetaleras (PIDRCAFÉ-UACH), Chapingo, Edo. de Méx., p. 1.
[2] Hannemann, Federico (1928). Datos prácticos sobre el Cultivo del Café, Librería Fausto de E. Wirth, México.

Fotography by Francisco J. Pérez Zúñiga

Fotography by Francisco J. Pérez Zúñiga

Fotography by Francisco J. Pérez Zúñiga

Fotography by Francisco J. Pérez Zúñiga

Fotography by Francisco J. Pérez Zúñiga

Fotography by Francisco J. Pérez Zúñiga

Fotography by Francisco J. Pérez Zúñiga

Fotography by Francisco J. Pérez Zúñiga

ones found halfway up. The larger the seed, the larger the cotyledon, thus the development of the plant within the seedbed will be larger. The seed has to be pulped, whether by hand or in the pulping machine, and has to be dried under a shade, where it can be in contact with the wind, so that its germinating potential can be preserved.

The first thing formed once the seed germinates is the root, next the stem, and then the first two leaves that, after disentangling, bloom, letting the parchment fall to the ground, that is, the parchment that covered the seed until then. The new plant is formed and, after strengthening itself for a while, is transplanted in the seedbed, where it remains approximately one year. In order to prepare the seedbed, Hannemann instructed "to form ridges of 1.20 centimeters wide and to place a thread next to them, setting small pegs every 30 centimeters with the intention of indicating the spot of the little plants; once planted, these trees could remain in the seedbed for several years". The new plant is considered ready to be taken to the plantation once it has its first couple of fruit branches, but it is preferred to wait until it has three of them, not sooner or later, since it could either be lost for being young or else there is a lot of root-cutting to do.

If the plantation is new, it must be weeded out and a shade must be established —that is, in most cases, since there are also plantations without shade— with the existing trees or by planting proper ones. Marks should then be placed to indicate the distance between coffee trees, depending on the type of soil, the setting of the land and the climate. The most common distances are 2 by 2 meters, 2.5 by 2.5 meters, and even up to 3 by 3 meters.

When dealing with coffee trees that are being sown again in an existing plantation, Hannemann recommended to proceed the same way as if there is fertile soil. In contrast, if the soil is poor, it is advisable to gather the black soil found on the surrounding surface and to use it to fill half of the hole designed for planting the coffee tree.

The next step is to select the healthiest plants, the ones with rich foliage, straight and thick stem, and to leave small seeds and weak plants out of the list. The coffee tree should then be transplanted to the plantation before its branches develop; there, with all necessary care, it will start producing within three to four years, reaching perhaps its maximum productivity stage at the age of ten, which will decrease after twenty years.

Types of crops in Mexico

In Mexico there are five different ways of producing coffee by considering the type of shading employed or its absence as one of its characteristics:

1. Rustic or montane. Coffee is grown under a great diversity of the existing shade trees of the locality, especially cloud forests and semi-deciduous forests. It is the most important type in Guerrero and Oaxaca, with over 70% of the total.

2. Traditional polyculture or coffee garden. Coffee is cultivated among many other useful plants, whether natural vegetation or introduced species. This is quite relevant in Veracruz, Chiapas and Puebla.

3. Commercial polyculture. Coffee is grown underneath shade trees that were introduced as leguminous plants (Inga spp) or fruit trees, for instance, citrus and timber-yielding trees.

4. Shade monoculture or specialized shade. This coffee is cultivated almost exclusively under shade trees of the genus Inga.

5. Full-sun or unshaded mono-culture. A coffee crop without tree shading, that is, directly cultivated under the sun. This is a production model with a high use of agrochemicals. It is found in Puebla and Veracruz .[3]

Four out of five of these systems –the ones with shading– have more biomass, nutrients, biodiversity, as well as more hydrological and microclimatic balance than the mono-cultural system or specialized coffee-growing, which gives them higher ecological stability. The high biodiversity these systems have avoids frequent plague outbreaks and reduces the use of pesticides and fertilizers (external supplies), making them more profitable.

Many coffee-growing areas for organic coffee derived from these production systems, especially the rustic and the traditional poly-culture ones.

The unshaded mono-cultural system expanded in areas like Xicotepec, Puebla, central Veracruz and Soconusco in Chiapas, imitating the experiences from Brazil, Hawaii, Costa Rica, El Salvador and Colombia. This system was well received in Xicotepec by both small and large producers, but the severe frosts of December 1989 damaged their crops and, as a consequence, several producers went back to the shade system, which reduced 10% of the crop in the region. With the exception of some high regions, the rest of the zones have experimented heavy losses.

The success of the unshaded mono-cultural system is related to the intensity of cultivation practices (weed control, pruning, and so on), phytosanitary protection, fertilization, high level agrochemical usage, high densities in coffee trees and the use of improved short-height varieties.

[3] With some variations, this relationship is included in the Master Plan of the system coffee product in Mexico, *op. cit.* y Barrera, Juan F. "Principios agroecológicos para el manejo de plagas en cafetales", en Pohlan, Jurgen, Editor (2002). *México y la cafeticultura chiapaneca. Reflexiones y alternativas para los cafeticultores*, Shaker Verlag, pp. 201-207.

Care-giving tasks involve regulating the shade, controlling the weeds, as well as cleaning and grading the plant: plague and disease control, pruning, trimming and fertilizing. Some tasks must be performed manually, although there have been some adaptations to small machines in order to speed up duties such as cleaning, pruning coffee trees and shade trees, as well as digging holes.

The shade

The most adequate tree for shading the coffee trees due to its characteristics belongs to the Inga family–that is, according to current studies, even though it was recommended by Hannemann back in 1928– and it is known by the name Cuajinicuil, also called cuje, chalúm or chalahuite. This tree never sheds its leaves and preserves its cool top lush during the whole year; its foliage never grows too thick; the trunk grows just enough, and the shape of the top is ideal for shading to the coffee shrub.

As for plantations with gentle slopes, banana trees provide good shading, not to say they help retain plenty of humidity within their trunks and loosen the soil with their long roots.

Cleanups

During the dry season, all weeds surrounding the coffee trees must be removed by cutting their roots, unless these are quite deep. As for the rainy season, it is necessary to clean the area in order to avoid having weeds covering the coffee trees. Removed herbs and weeds should be spread out on the ground either far away from the coffee trees or close to them, depending on how humid or dry, respectively, the area is. In general terms, plantations require three cleanings per year: one during the dry time of the year and the other two during the rainy season. A total of two cleanups suffice when the climate is dry and the plantation well shaded.

In regard to manual cleaning control, 80% of the producers use machetes; the number of times they do it varies in between one to three times per year. Hoe usage constitutes 6.3%, and chemical control represents 8.11%.[4]

[4] Data from 2005 included in the master plan of the coffee system-product in Mexico, *op. cit*

Fertilization

A coffee tree requires the following nutritious elements in order to develop properly: carbon, oxygen and hydrogen, which are subtracted from water and air, and Nitrogen, Phosphorus and Potassium, called micronutrients. The plant also needs, in a lesser degree, two more groups of elements: calcium, magnesium and sulfur, known as secondary elements, and, finally, the micronutrients group: boron, copper, iron, manganese, molybdemun, zinc and chlorine.

When there is a lack of one of these elements, the plant is prone to get sick and to decrease the quality of the production. Therefore, it is important to keep a balance of these nutrients. It is necessary to counterbalance any deficiency found in the plants with fertilization, so they can stay healthy.

There are two types of fertilizers: agrochemical and organic. As expected, the former ones are made by specialized companies, while the latter are developed by the producers themselves, who use the coffee pulp obtained from processing plants along with cane residue, several types of cow, horse, donkey and goat manure, and green and dry plant material processed in composts or vermicomposts. Actually, vermicomposting is an alternative way to help improve the microbiological characteristics of organic waste, and it also reduces pollution problems generated by solid organic waste; it also regenerates the soil, among other advantages.

Artificial fertilizers are not necessary for properly shaded plantations and for those in good conditions, although it could be profitable to better off the production. Fertilizers should be distributed around each coffee tree, keeping a 30 centimeters

distance from the trunk and burying them 2 centimeters deep to keep them from being dragged away by water. It should be considered that the circle gets placed right underneath the extreme part of the branches, since the extreme parts of the roots are found at that same distance.

The effect of fertilization can also be observed in the appearance and quality of the coffee in a cup: an excess of nitrogen decreases the density of the bean and increases the content of caffeine, while an excess of potassium shows bad appearance due to insufficient coloring, something that can also happen when there was a deficiency of magnesium. Consequently, any excess, deficiency or lack of nutritional balance affects the quality of a cup of coffee. ·

Pruning and trimming the coffee tree

Pruning and trimming require constant work in the plantation, but these tasks can be done as part of the *"agobio"*[5] practice, which is performed in order to take care of the coffee tree when it reaches a height of 1.25 to 1.50 meters. The *agobio* process consists in bending the plant to the point where the upper part of the trunk remains almost horizontal and its lower part slightly inclined; the plant is thus kept tied to a peg. Several buds will sprout on the sloping parts of the trunk after some weeks. The buds must be selected once they reach a size of 20 to 30 centimeters long: the ones to preserve should remain there while the others should be pulled out. The *agobio* practice helps to obtain some buds so the coffee tree can be composed of four to six main stems, without letting it grow, facilitating the harvest and not having fruit branches obstructing the way.

As it happens every year, new buds will appear once or twice and should be rid with the intention of keeping the shape given to the plant. Thus, the need of pruning the plant will be avoided. However, if the branches break, it is important to cut them from the trunk of the tree; this must be done carefully so that there isn't any remnant or any scratched and cut branch, since humidity accumulates in them and can cause them to rot.

[5] Hannemann, *op. cit.*

HARVESTING

"The quality of a cup of coffee depends not only on the growing site and edafoclimatic conditions [soil quality, rainfall, temperature, solar radiation, shade regulation and overall effect of altitude on weather variables], but also on a good harvest and the proper processing of the bean".[1]

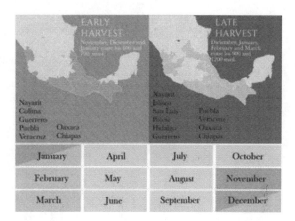

Harvesting has to be done quickly, thus requiring a lot of workforce. Cherry picking in coffee farms accounts for 40 - 60% of the production cost. Several *prunings* are needed depending on the maturity state as well as the concentration of fruits; in the first pruning also called *pepena*, all ripe, dry and bad fruits are collected; in the next pruning only ripe fruits are picked and in the last pruning known as *arrase*, all remaining fruits are collected including the greens and those not yet ripe or *pintones*. The latter and those obtained from *pepena* are processed separately.

There are four or five flowering periods for coffee plantations located along the Gulf of Mexico, whereas for those along the Pacific there are only one or two. January and February account for 55% of total domestic production. Usually, harvesting is marked by the altitude of the producing region, running from September to December in low regions (250 to 800 MASL), from November to January in middle regions (800 to 1,200 MASL) and from December to April in high regions (1,200 to 1,500 MASL).

Harvesting is carried out by hand, therefore concentrating job creation in coffee regions. Cherries must be processed before reaching 12 hours after the picking.

Participation of the natives is indeed quite relevant. In 2005 The Guiding Plan for Coffee Product System had calculated they are majority in 94 municipalities of the coffee region and 25% of the population in other 106 municipalities.

[1] Rodas R., César Augusto. "El beneficiado del café", in Pohlan, Jurgen, *op. cit.*, pp. 303-309.

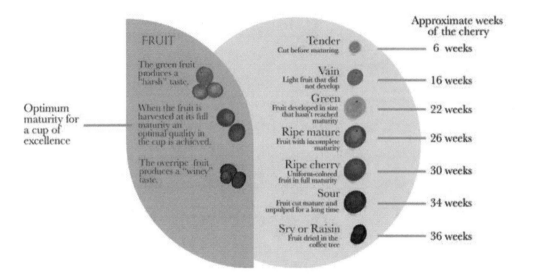

		Approximate weeks of the cherry
FRUIT	**Tender** Cut before maturing	6 weeks
The green fruit produces a "harsh" taste.	**Vain** Light fruit that did not develop	16 weeks
When the fruit is harvested at its full maturity an optimal quality in the cup is achieved.	**Green** Fruit developed in size that hasn't reached maturity	22 weeks
	Ripe mature Fruit with incomplete maturity	26 weeks
The overripe fruit produces a "winey" taste.	**Ripe cherry** Uniform-colored fruit in full maturity	30 weeks
	Sour Fruit cut mature and unpulped for a long time	34 weeks
	Sry or Raisin Fruit dried in the coffee tree	36 weeks

Optimum maturity for a cup of excellence

PROCESSING

Coffee processing includes a series of operations aimed at removing the natural casing of the seeds: pulp, mucilage, parchment and silverskin, as well as improving its appearance. This can be done in two ways: the wet or the dry methods.

The wet method, which includes wet and dry processing stages for either parchment or washed coffee, is performed on coffee classified as washed and has five steps:

1. Pulp removal (pulping).
2. Mucilage break (fermentation).
3. Washing.
4. Parchment coffee drying.
5. Milling and Grading.

In order to obtain a good quality coffee, it must be ensured that only ripe fruit reaches processing

The steps listed above are divided in two phases: wet processing (steps 1, 2, 3) and dry processing (4 y 5). In dry processing, moisture is removed directly from cherries thus obtaining the bola or *capulin* coffee, which is generated from natural coffee. In this method, fresh fruits undergo three operations:

1. Cherry drying.
2. Removal of dried coverings through a single mechanical operation.
3. Milling and Grading.[1]

Wet processing

Wet processing has been modified thanks to technological innovation. There are now pulping machines (coffee pulpers) that, depending on the materials of which they are made (steel or cupper sleeves, molten steel disks) and also on their size, are capable of pulping from 40 up to 3 thousand Kg. per hour. Moreover, there are mucilage machines ranging from lower to higher performance and some are even capable of doing without fermentation and avoid the excessive use of water in this processing stage.

In Mexico, development of agrobusiness is rather diverse, partly due to capitalization and access to credit to acquire state of the art machinery, but also because some procedures, such as fermentation, are regarded as tradition and hence benefits are attributed to them, which reflect later in the product quality. Still, it is possible to find plots of land where little electric or manual pulpers are used, at the same time, we see producers within the same area showing much bigger processing capacity, who are however utilizing machinery and techniques that are over twenty years old.

One of the most traditional coffee processing methods still used in certain regions is described as follows. This method begins by soaking the cherry in water; when done in a formal fashion processing relies on siphons equipped with a mesh or a strainer in the upper side, where foreign materials mixed with cherries, like leaves or twigs, get caught up.

Fruits remaining at the bottom are good quality cherries and those floating around are bad quality ones, composed of dried, empty and some green beans; finally these have to be pulped and fermented separately since they are not of good quality.

---

[1] Classification presented by Bello Mendoza, Ricardo. "Impacto ambiental del beneficiado húmedo del café", in Pohlan, Jurgen (ed.), *México y la cafeticultura chiapaneca. Reflexiones y alternativas para los cafeticultores*, Shaker Verlag, 2002, pp 311-320.

Hydraulic reception and coffee pulping system

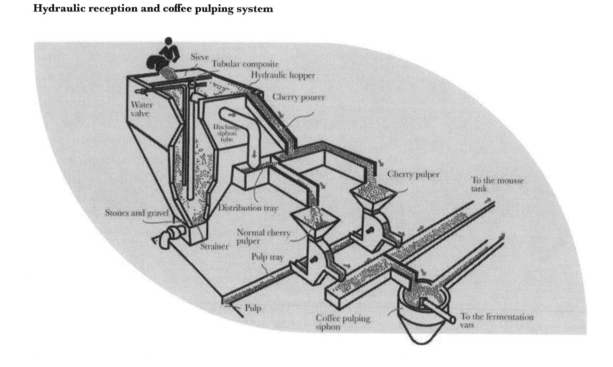

Immediately, or the morning after at the latest, pulping is done, in order to prevent fermentation from affecting taste. Coffee pulpers must be in the best conditions to avoid damage to cherries, as they arrive in different sizes and change depending on the harvest season: the first and last prunings provide smaller cherries and that is why pulpers have to be adjusted according to the season.

Pulping is carried out with either cylinder or disk machines that are well adjusted so the beans don't get through with the pulp nor are "bitten". To obtain a product of good appearance and quality it is necessary to stir the cherry steadily until surface water is gone.

Pulped cherries are then taken to another tank for fermentation, allowing the remaining covering to molder. Typically, fermentation takes between 30 and 48 hours depending on the region, though if too dry, it could take up to 70 hours. Afterwards, cherries are washed in the same tank or in a bigger one. For small labors, washing is done in the fermentation tank, stirring the cherries with a paddle until floating materials such as empty seeds and pulps are separated and ready to be set aside manually, mead is thrown away several times and replaced with clean water until it is again clean altogether.

In large plantations where traditional system is still maintained, mechanical washing is done with centrifugal pumps that allow immediate mucilage detachment, then it is sent running by canals (*correteo*), here sorting based on density occurs, separating those of first class, second class and chuff or *natas* .[2]

Once washed, beans are let to fall down into the sundeck or patio when in small plantations, while in large plantations they are dried mechanically. Proper temperatures range from 60 to 75 degrees Celsius. Wet processing for washed coffees, regardless of the method being used for obtaining parchments, ends with coffee drying.

Once dried, beans are ready for sale, but if they are intended for storing under wet weather for several months, or if shipped on a long trip, they will need a little extra drying and

be put through another machine to remove parchment and tissue, then polished, put through a fan and finally through a sorting machine where sorted into five to seven types.

Dry processing is intended to prepare beans for roasting and consumption. It is used to obtain non-washed coffees such as capulin or bola, and during the complementary part of

[2] Natas (chuff) are green, empty or dried beans as well as any other lightweight materials.

washed coffees in the parchment phase on their way to green or gold coffee. Processing goes through the following stages: maturation of parchment coffee, parchment cleaning, hulling or threshing, bean sorting, *catadoras*, *desmanche*, weighing and packing.

Parchment maturation is about stacking and storing of parchment in silos or hoppers until a humidity of between 11% and 13% is reached; by cleaning –by hand or with machines– all junk like nails, rubbish, stones, nuts, metal chunks, twigs,

leaves, etc. is removed; hulling –done by different methods, most of them mechanical– is about removing parchment or endocarp from the seeds.

Bean sorting

Sorting of beans is done according to shape and size, technical basis vary depending on whether the bean is "flat-convex" or "snail". So according to its shape and size, bean is named as follows:

- Normal Bean or *planchuela*, a typical bean of convex flattened shape that resembles the half of an ellipse.

- Triangle, a bean with two flattened sides and one convex side, normally three in each fruit.

- Giant, these beans are bigger than the normal type, showing multiple creases on parchment and little corneal substance, which makes them quite light in weight, it is possible to find one normal bean and one giant together in the same fruit; it is sometimes named "elephant" or "monster".

- Snail, an egg-shaped, snail-like bean; the other seed inside the fruit develops freely taking the round shape of the fruit.

- *Vano* (empty), a seemingly normal bean having little of no corneal substance, which makes it float in the water.

In the *catadoras* (initial selection) stage, defective beans are removed by cleaning coffee beans and complementing the work of classifiers to improve their efficiency. *Desmanche* (final selection) is done in sorting machines capable of removing black, off-color and cracked beans. Finally, coffee gold is weighed and packed in 69 Kg. bags equal to 1.5 hundredweights, ready to be distributed in centers of consumption.

ORGANIC COFFEE

ORGANIC COFFEE

To start this type of farming, soil where conventional techniques have been applied may be utilized, in this case the conversion period needed to make use of organic techniques could take from 12 to 36 months, depending on the kind of fertilizers, insecticides and other chemical agents; or plantations starting with this technique.

Areas reserved for growing organic coffee (seedbed, nursery and plantation) must be chemical free; sometimes such areas are found to be next to conventional farmings. In this situation, organic farming manuals advise on creating natural barriers: growing ornamental plants or diversified farming that could even contribute to increasing economic income.

Fertilizer, widely used on plants in orchards and on bushes in plantations to provide the required nutrients, is produced for the same manufacturers with organic matter, a feature that also helps in saving production costs. [1]

[1] Solabac Cuacua, José Ciro and Lucino Sosa Maldonado, *Manual de café orgánico*, México, Universidad Autónoma de Chapingo/Yeni Navan-Michizá, 2010.

Shade is very important for this type of farming, as it contributes with the following advantages:

a) Prevents excesive deforestation.
b) Protects soil from rain and promotes a better water filtration.
c) Reduces drastic changes in temperature.
d) Helps in undergrowth control.
e) Increases soil fertility.
f) Reduces plague attack by creating a diverse environment that promotes harmful insect dispersion and fosters development of beneficial insect species. [2]

[2] INCA Rural, Consejo Mexicano del Café, *Manual para la Cafeticultura Mexicana. Cuaderno 5. Cultivo Orgánico del Cafeto*, México, 1997.

There are many techniques to keep plantations and coffee farms free from plagues and pests. In this regard there is no big difference with conventional farming. Here too a lot of workforce is needed and, just as advised to every producer, the best cherries should be selected keeping them from mixing with green fruits, as these contain a high degree of tannins which affect the taste of coffee quite negatively, making it astringent, namely bitter. Though another selection can be done during wet processing, it is better to strive for getting good results in every quality checkpoint.[3]

Organic coffee processing is comparable to that performed on other types of coffee. Nevertheless, environmental logic suggests relying on processes that employ machines with a minimal water consumption. It is important to highlight here the environmental benefit of the pulping stage where drying is done directly by mechanical means and leaves out fermentation. Even one single machine can be used for both pulping and washing, instead of using the so valued liquid first in the canals for pulping and then in fermentation tanks, besides washing the bean with an extra amount of water.

In addition to product certification, organic coffee farmers seek other certifications related to their processes such as neutral carbon emissions, by lessening their power consumption in order to reduce greenhouse gas emission.

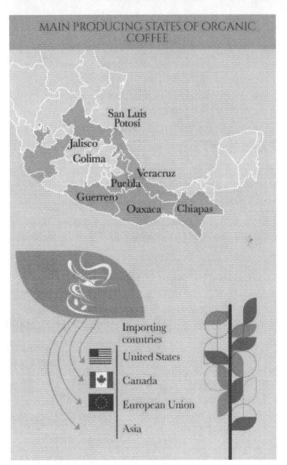

MAIN PRODUCING STATES OF ORGANIC COFFEE

San Luis Potosí

Jalisco
Colima

Veracruz
Puebla
Guerrero
Oaxaca   Chiapas

Importing countries
United States
Canada
European Union
Asia

---

[3] Durán Ramírez, Felipe, "Café orgánico", in *Cultivo del Café*, Colombia, Grupo Latino Editores, 2009.

STORAGE

STORAGE

Coffee can be stored in parchment or in gold, packed in bags, in bulk or in silos. When packed in bags, the piles or *tongas* are placed on 30 pallets cm over the floor. For ventilation purposes, piles must not lean on the warehouse walls. Each *tonga* is made up of 20 to 25 bags.

Coffee storage is an opportunity to measure and homogenize the amount of moisture in different beans by transferring moisture from the wettest beans to the driest ones, which is

achieved after a 30-day period. This is how long stored coffee can stay free of notorious deterioration, with a moisture level between 25 al 30% and with, needless to say, a good ventilation to help it complete the drying process.

Once dry, stored beans must be kept in a humidity no greater than 10 to 12%, otherwise any increase might produce spots of raise in temperature facilitating mold formation that taints the bean and carries bad taste over to the cup.

ROASTING AND GRINDING

ROASTING AND GRINDING

Roasting

Industry in the final stage focuses on producing five products: Roasted and Ground coffee, Decaffeinated, Extracts, Soluble Coffee and Lyophilized Coffee (dehydration process using freeze-drying for maximum preservation of food properties).

Prior to its preparation in any form, coffee has to go through the roasting process, during which the characteristic aroma

will be developed. Before roasting, green coffee can be kept in this state for several years.

When roasted, the bean develops new compounds that account for 30% of its weight after roasting, those being caramel, carbon dioxide and other 700 compounds that comprise the volatile aromas formed by Maillard reactions (named after the discoverer) which start around 160 degrees and last until the roasting stops.

When the final temperature of roasting increases, aromas increase and decrease experiencing a variation of the acidity level (when it comes to coffee, acidity should be understood as mildness, not as ph) and bitterness in taste, it increases with temperature as acidity decreases; the more subtle the roast, the higher the acidity, and the more intense the roast is, the bitter the taste; a light roast reduces weight loss but does not allow coffee to develop its volatile aromas through Maillard reactions; moreover it reduces the amount of trigonelline and fatty acids, both of which are perceived in coffee, causing a bitter, unpleasant and little digestive taste.

There is no doubt that the ideal roast depends on the likes of consumers, although according to tasters "in order to evaluate coffee quality, a light roast should be used".[2]

---

[1] "El arte del tostado", that is how Avelino Hernández calls it, and from whom the following notes are taken as he refers the topic in the book *La cultura de tomar café. Guía para estimular el gusto por el buen café*, published by Confederación Mexicana de Productores de Café (s/f).
[2] Katzeff, Paul, El manifiesto de los catadores de café, EUA, Thanksgiving Coffe Company, 2001.

RELATION NO. ACTRON AND CHARACTERISTICS OF FLAVOR IN THE COFFEE	
Description of the toast	Characteristics
Light toast	Color 60 to 65 or higher, little intense, like not fully developed aroma.
Medium toast	Color 55 to 60 soft aroma, acid, like original product, light body. Little suitable for espresso.
Medium	Color 50 to 55 aroma more intense, somewhat bitter taste will start but keeps a good balance.
Medium high	Color 45 to 50 aroma very intense, but losing nuances, bitter, high body.
Dark	Color 40 to 45 it begins to notice something burnt aromas and pronounced sour taste, it loses acidity, but can work well in places where like the strong coffee.
Very dark	Less than 40 loses aroma. It is clear many oils, the taste is clearly burned.

Tomado de la revista Fórum Café, núm. 37, España, 2009

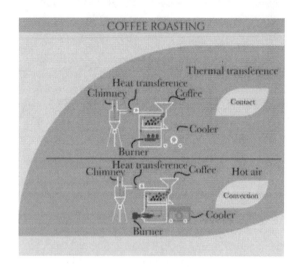

COFFEE ROASTING

The following table for commercial use allows differentiating some of the features in accordance to the roast level. This table is based on Agtron/Specialty Coffee Association of America's 8-color disks system that refer to the same number of roast levels.

Roasting machines reach up to 400° C, at this temperature the essential oils are released together with that delicious taste acclaimed all over the world. The relevance of this stage in the whole process has taken specialization and professionalism to a higher ground, put to test at various international competitions.

Roasting is done in three stages: In the first one moisture in coffee is reduced from its initial point of approximately 12/14 % down to 3/4 %, in the second stage the bean is expanded producing gas and in the third stage the required taste is acquired.[3]

When roasting has come to an end, coffee must be cooled fast to lessen the loss of volatile compounds and retain as much as possible inside the beans. Once under ambient temperature, coffee is sent to warehouses to rest between eight and twelve hours before final packing (this is not necessary if packing ground coffee).

This step of the process is important to fully develop coffee's organoleptic and aromatic properties. When resting time is over, coffee has to be packed immediately whether as beans or ground coffee.

Grinding

The size of particles in ground coffee has an influence on good organoleptic properties found in a cup of coffee.

[3] Solà, Albert, *La ruta del Café*, Barcelona, EDICAT, 2002.

Light roast.

Medium light roast.

Medium roast.

Medium high roast.

Dark roast.

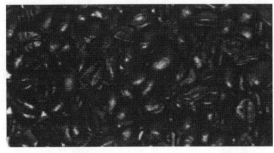

Very dark roast.

GRIND DEGREE FOR DIFFERENT TYPES OF COFFEE MACHINES

GRIND	COFFEE MACHINE		TYPE OF COFFEE PREPARED
1. Coarse	De Olla		De olla Americano
2. Medium-coarse	French press Percolator		Americano
3. Medium	Chemex Siphon or Kona Drip Pots		Americano
4. Fine	Moka or Italian		Espresso
	Espresso Coffee capsules		Espresso
5. Extra fine	Turkish		Turkish

"Beverage preparation seeks to extract the components from a granular bed of coffee by the action of hot water during a fixed time of contact. The bigger the size of the particles the smaller the area of contact between water and coffee, and the beverage produced can result either light or under-extracted. A bed comprised of too tiny particles will render a larger area of contact and beverage may turn out dark or over-extracted".[4]

Medium grind.

Extra fine grind.

Medium-coarse roast.

Fine grind.

Coarse roast.

[4] Guevara-Barreto y Castaño-Castrillón, "Caracterización granulométrica del café colombiano tostado y molido", thesis presented at Universidad de Colombia to attain the degree of Chemical Engineer, 2005.

EXTRACT, SOLUBLE, DECAFFEINATED AND OTHERS

EXTRACT, SOLUBLE, DECAFFEINATED AND OTHERS

Extracts

In 1966 Panamanian Juan Alberto Morales patented in Madrid a "process for producing extract of liquid coffee". The inventor argued that existing processes for instant coffee production altered its taste so badly that coffee tasted "more like a substitute". The right thing to do, he explained in the patent, was to rely on a process that prevented: "1) A variation in taste as a result of raw beans going across the sea. 2) Defects of roasting linked to ash generation. 3) That all loss occurred in milling and packing was over. 4) That during coffee preparation the kitchen was free from factors posing a negative impact on coffee taste".

In their process, beans were roasted using microwaves or infra red ray, "that makes beans even and deep, both on the crust and on the inside in equal extent, allowing the adjustment of wave or ray intensity to avoid ash generation".

Nowadays, there are different processes to make extracts and many of these are applied to soluble production, but they are also utilized in the kitchen to aromatize a variety of dishes and it is even possible to make it at home blending two spoons of broken or grinded beans with half a cup of water and half a cup of vodka and then let to rest for 6 to 8 weeks, stirring once a week.

Soluble

In 1900 Japanese chemist Satori Kato patented in Chicago the process to produce instant coffee. Years later, "English man George C. Washington, while he was living in Guatemala invented the first instant coffee that was later produced at industrial scale. Although the taste of this type of coffee was not certainly the best it was well received, especially among soldiers in the front during World War I".

Soluble coffee is the granulated powder of coffee extract once water is removed. The elaboration of 1 kg of this type of coffee "requires a lesser amount of Robusta coffee as raw material than the amount required if Arabica were used, hence it is rather exceptional to find in the market 100% Arabica soluble coffee ".

In order to remove water from the extract, procedures such as atomization drying are utilized, this works at temperatures between 40 and 50° C and under pressures lower than atmospheric, this way atomization is performed "as on a high tower, and by the time it reaches the bottom water has evaporated almost entirely and only the powder of soluble coffee remains"; also the lyophilization process consists of freezing the extract at temperatures lower than 50 degrees below zero to prevent loss of aroma and other features which are valued in coffee beverages." Even though lyophilization process is more expensive and complex than atomization drying, the rate of lyophilized coffee has raised due to consumers' demand for higher quality".

[1] Durán Ramírez, Felipe, *Cultivo del Café*, Colombia, Grupo Latino Editores, 2009.

In October 2011 the first lyophilization plant was inaugurated in Mexico. The company Ecom Agroindustrial Corporation, based in Sweden, through its subsidiary in Mexico, Agroindustrias Unidas de México (AMSA), convened investors interested in this project and two companies answered, one from Japan (Key Coffee), and the second from Spain (Prosol.) The plant, located in Puerto Madero, gave origin to the creation of Specialty Coffees of Chiapas, S.A.P.I de C.V. (CAFESCA), in March 2009. This proposal was supported by the state and federal governments that provided the necessary foundation to attract the private investment required for the consolidation of the project".[2]

It is important to clarify that between 1975-1976, the Mexican Institute of Coffee elaborated the first study of feasibility and profitability of the lyophilization plant, to be established in Puerto Madero, Chiapas, creating for such effect the company promoter of the project, which was delayed due to several conflicted interests.

Decaffeinated

Currently, several processes are carried out to decaffeinate. The first and most widespread is through chemical solvents. The most effective and popular solvents used in green coffee beans are Methylene chloride (DCM) and ethyl acetate (EA). "Caffeine is extracted from the previously wetted green coffee beans through successive extractions until virtual elimination of caffeine is achieved. Then the beans are treated with steam to remove the solvent… which is recovered by distillation and reused for further extractions. The process ends with coffee drying by hot air to reach the initial moisture".[3]

Decaffeination by pressurized steam comprises the following steps:

- Water extraction from previously wetted coffee beans.
- Separation of caffeine from the liquid extract obtained.
- Concentration of caffeine free aqueous solution at 10-30%.
- Reabsorption of this concentrated aqueous solution over decaffeinated grains .[4]

A process derived from the latter can be performed with a caffeine-free green coffee extract, when coffee beans are introduced in the solvent caffeine leaves the bean the other components do not. This chemical phenomenon is called osmosis and through it are minimized the losses of soluble solids that contain the organoleptic characteristics.

The third process is known as supercritical fluid decaffeination: CO_2. "The process begins with the extraction of green coffee beans previously soaked in CO_2. This fluid gradually becomes enriched in caffeine. Subsequently the CO_2 solution passes

Fotography taken of CAFESCA, Chiapas, Mexico.

[2] Information obtained from the CAFESCA website (http://www.cafesca.com).
[3] Blasco Carmen, "Café descafeinado", Paper presented in theI XXI Spanish Congress of Coffee, Santiago de Compostela. In the magazine Fórum del Café, núm. 18, pp. 6-15. Barcelona, 2004.
[4] Ibid., p. 8.
[5] Ibid., p. 9.

through activated carbon, which retains caffeine and allows the recuperation of CO_2 for reuse. The process ends with the drying of the beans through conventional methods".[5]

In Mexico there has been several decaffeinators. The possibility of a caffeine-free bush is something that has been brought up since the 1970s. In our country, agronomists of INMECAFE announced, since then, the location of a coffee tree with this characteristic. And the same findings, thirty years later, have been discovered analyzing wild species of shrubs in Madagascar and Ethiopia. So far there are no crops that have transferred this property to commercial varieties, however, with the current knowledge on the coffee genome, new expectations about decaffeinated coffee trees arise.

Universities in Hawaii, United Kingdom, and Japan, among others, have studied the matter, of which the International Coffee Organization gave account in the Seminar Genetically Modified Coffee, held in London on May 17, 2005.

Other products

Creativity and charm for its taste have propelled the creation of multiple beverages based on coffee. Wine, yogurt, cookies, jam, bread, candy and even cosmetics contain extracts or concentrates intended to take advantage of the aroma and taste of roasted coffee bean. Those covered with chocolate are truly an exquisite candy. Everyday, supermarkets, gyms or kiosks at bus stations, are including more and more products related to rubiacea. It is now clear that coffee is not just the beverage that has conquered the world, but also its aroma, taste and properties exert an attraction difficult to compare to any other natural product.

Chocolate covered roasted coffee. Fotography by Enrique Cantú Garza

[6] *Ibid.*, pp. 12-13.

EXTRACT, SOLUBLE, DECAFFEINATED AND OTHERS

QUALITIES OF COFFEE

QUALITIES OF COFFEE

Coffee quality is determined by natural variations and the care of man. In plantations, factors like rainfall, sunlight and relative humidity influence the development of the fruit. Water, carbohydrates, fats, proteins, alkaloids and minerals stay in the fruit for seven and a half months, which is the average time required for ripening, divided in four stages. In the first month and a half development is minimum; in the next two months it will reach full size, seeds will contain 85% water and 15% solid compounds, if water is insufficient, green fruit will fall down; in the third stage, which lasts two and a half months, the volume of the fruit will increase, water and solid ratio will get balance, if water runs short cherries blacken; during the last stage, which takes one and a half months, husk and mucilage develop; the green in the fruit turns red and aromatic substances are formed.[1]

Weather and care provided to bushes have an influence on the healthy growth of the fruit and therefore, on the quality of beans. Greenness and brightness of the plants are an indicator of the health of the coffee farm. During harvesting, the intense red of the cherries is key to selecting the best fruits.

In both wet and dry processing, the cherry is pulped and its moisture is reduced. In order to ensure the quality, moisture should not be above 12%, if this requirement is not met, then coffee loses its properties and development of mold and bacteria increases. When green coffee is obtained, other features may be valued based on aroma and coloration. The smell of coffee should always be fresh and neat, inappropriate smell of green coffees reveal over-fermentation or contamination by mold or soil. It is possible to identify degrees of moisture by sight, beans containing

[1] Castañeda Párraga, Enrique, *Bases potenciales. De la chacra cafetalera diversificada y amigable con el medio ambiente*, Perú, Tecnatrop, 2004.

6-12% moisture are dark gray, those with 14-15% are white, bluish green ones have 12-13%, greens 10-11%, light greens 9% and if any pale or yellowish is seen, that would mean they have under 8%.

In storage and transportation of green bean, high levels of humidity must be avoided in order to keep a good quality. Roast classes determine new qualities of coffee; in this process the bean goes from green to yellow tones and then to brown. Heat applied will alter the taste and aroma of beans, oils released here will enhance the taste, which may vary within a few seconds if exposed to high temperatures. Types of ground coffee will allow another variation. There is no specific type of ground coffee to choose from to get the best coffee beverage, it all depends on the desired type to be tasted and this is not the last step when defining quality. Water quality and brewing time are involved too. And what is the best process and time to get and drink a nice cup of coffee?

SOME PESTS, DISEASES, AND DEFECTS OF COFFEE IN MEXICO

SOME PESTS, DISEASES, AND DEFECTS
OF COFFEE IN MEXICO

Pests

According to a survey of coffee producers[1], 81.23% report presence of pests in their plantations, with 44.7% of borer. By feeding directly from the fruit, coffee borer beetle affects considerably the quality of beans, lessening cherry coffee yield.

Coffee borer came to America since 1913 through Brazil. In Mexico the fact did not pose any real concern until 1971, when it reached Guatemala, then special care was taken to prevent pest from spreading, but in 1978 it was found for the

Hypothenemus hampei Ferrari.

first time in a coffee farm in Tuxtla Chico, Chiapas, near the border of Guatemala. Since then it continued to spread, first among coffee farms in Chiapas and across the country in the following years.

The battle against coffee borer beetle can't be by chemical control, since other coexisting crops might be affected. Often a better solution is trap installation, where the bug gets killed. Also, damaged cherries are carefully collected and at the end all cherries fallen to the ground are picked up too, soaking them in hot water later on to destroy both the bug and larvae. In 1988, the Colegio de la Frontera Sur (ECOSUR) brought from Africa the parasite *Cephalonomia stephanoderis*, whose only guest is the coffee borer, capable of an effective settling in those coffee farms where it got released. Considering the mortality of the insect, due to "fruit disposal during harvesting as well as low availability of stages of borer development prone to parasitation in periods of intercropping", the recommendation is to release large amounts of parasites per hectare, "which implies a massive growing and proper procedures for storage, transportation and release at the fields".[2]

Diseases

There are diseases caused by excess of humidity, which most of the time is explained by lack of ventilation produced when the distance between plantations is not adequate in relation to the density of bushes, or due to heavy shade or insufficient cleaning at plantations.

According to the aforementioned survey, 80.4% of coffee farmers reported the presence of diseases caused by fungus, standing out: *ojo de gallo*, rust, *mal de hilachas* (blackening) and anthracnose. Coffee rust, provoked by fungus Hemileia *vastatrix* and *ojo de gallo* cause defoliation and produce a relative fruit overload, preventing full development of the bean. Rust survives in the leaves of species Typica, Bourbon, Caturra, Mundo Novo and Catauaí, of the type Coffea Arabica. Rust cycle is regarded as incomplete, with one single host and a single form of reproductive organs, sick leaves from previous season become the main source of contamination when rain time begins.

Rust is present in every producing country and is well known since 1869. The first record of sick plants is that made by Europeans in Ceylon, now Sri Lanka. In the third quarter of the nineteenth century, Ceylon was a British colony with

[1] *Idem.*
[2] Gómez Ruiz, Jaime, "Efectividad de parasitoides para combatir a la broca", *Ecofronteras*, 4 (No. 12), 2000, p. 10.

Leaf damaged by mushroom

a worldwide-recognized coffee production. Rust brought that activity to an end and according to chronicles of the time, coffee had to be replaced with tea in order to keep the economy going, a situation that helped fondness of English people for the beverage.

In 1970 rust reached Brazil, appearing later in Mexico in Tapachula, Chiapas, in 1981. The intensity of the attack varies depending on weather and the type of coffee. Also, temperature and low altitude stimulate the activity of the disease. In Costa Rica during 1989/1990 and in Nicaragua 1995/1996 the presence of fungus had disastrous effects. According to researchers of ECOSUR,[3] the rust issue was underrated by Latin American governments over the decades of 1980 and 1990. From 2008 through 2011 strong attacks were reported in Colombia and in the period of 2010 to 2012 a case of severe attack appeared in Central America. In 2012 in Mexico, an "atypical" outbreak caused death to bushes and plants. The answer from the Federal Government was the execution of the "Emerging Program for Rust Control" across 22 municipalities in Soconusco and the Chiapas Sierra.

"More than 50 thousand kilograms of copper oxychloride fungicide were sprinkled over 58 thousand hectares property of roughly 23,500 producers.[4] The Cooperative Program for Protection and Modernization of Coffee Production and the Inter American Institute for Agriculture Cooperation (PROMECAFE-IICA) had calculated that in Central America, in the cycle 2012/2013, "rust caused a loss of 20% in production, 500 million dollars less in exportations and unemployment for half million people".

The way this plague has been fought is through fungicides, whereas the renovation of coffee farms with resistant materials is recommended as a preventive action. In Colombia for instance, researchers at the National Federation of Coffee Producers, with the support from the National Center for Coffee Research (CENICAFE), "have enabled the coffee producers to have varieties resistant to rust"[5], such as Variedad Castillo.

Coffee Defects

From cultivation stage to storage, beans may experience diverse damage that affect the taste of a cup of coffee. These harmful effects don't depend on the species' intrinsic properties, nor on the variety or environmental conditions, but on the good execution of picking, processing, sorting, milling and beverage preparation processes.

Bean damage is classified in field damage (damage by borer, amber bean, elephant bean, shell and body, etc.), field damage (blackened bean, dun bean, bean with silverskin, etc.), process damage (bean threshed by pulpers, smashed or cracked bean, fetid bean, etc.), storing damage.[6]

[3] Barrera, *et al.*, "La roya del café, crónica de una devastación anunciada", in *Ecofronteras*, 18(No. 49), 2013, pp. 22-25.
[4] *Ibid.*, p. 25.
[5] CropLife Latin America, s/f.
[6] Taken from Cantú and Mushinske, La Guía de defectos del café, México, United Nations Coffe Company, 2004[6]

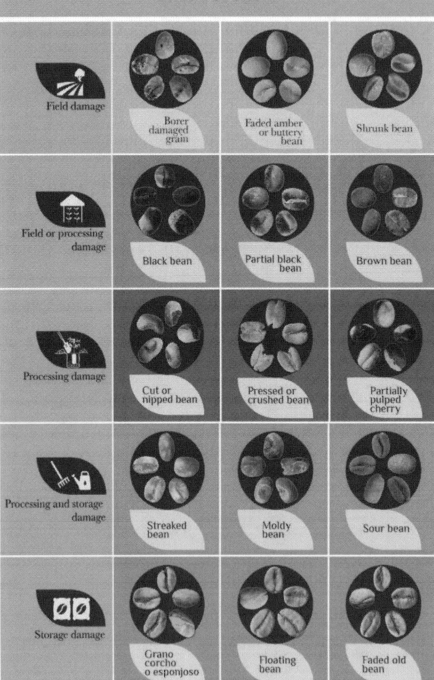

DEFECTS OF COFFEE

Field damage
- Borer damaged grain
- Faded amber or buttery bean
- Shrunk bean

Field or processing damage
- Black bean
- Partial black bean
- Brown bean

Processing damage
- Cut or nipped bean
- Pressed or crushed bean
- Partially pulped cherry

Processing and storage damage
- Streaked bean
- Moldy bean
- Sour bean

Storage damage
- Grano corcho o esponjoso
- Floating bean
- Faded old bean

NOT ONLY EXQUISITE, BUT HEALTHY

NOT ONLY EXQUISITE, BUT HEALTHY

In 1693, French physician Philipe Sylvestre Dufour wrote his Treaty on Coffee, Tea and Chocolate, in which he described the virtues of coffee, and towards the turn of the century "a Parisian physician prescribed coffee enemas to relax large intestine and refresh the skin".[1]

By mid 18th century, Diderot and D'Alembert included in their Encyclopedia a description of the benefits of coffee on treating obesity and headaches. Caffeine, the main component of coffee, was first isolated in 1820 by German chemist Friedlieb Ferdinand, which originated a series of further studies.

In 2003, during a seminar organized by the International Coffee Organization in Cartagena, doctor Beatriz Londoño, who was then general director of the Colombian Institute of Family Welfare, highlighted that there were at least 19 thousand written works on the effects of coffee on human body. Moreover, she added "sensitivity to caffeine depends on many factors, such as frequency and amount of intake, as well as weight and physical condition of the individual. Also, on variety, grinding, processing or preparation method".

That is why it is not easy to summarize or be categorical on this subject. Science is based upon data seeking the truth. However, such data are conditioned to the features of the sample they are extracted from. This is not about questioning every single research made, but rather about conferring their grain of truth. The following studies gather information from both Mexican and international academics that got the samples, observed reactions of the human body and analyzed

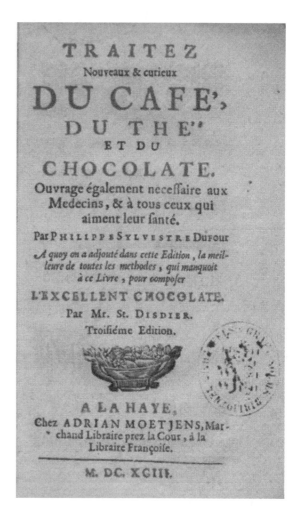

---

[1] Pendergrast, Mark, *El café, historia de la semilla que cambió el mundo*, Spain, Javier Vergara Publisher, 2002, p. 30.

the collected data. Coffee is beneficial for human health. Every man and woman is responsible for knowing the effects of coffee in their own bodies and drink just the number of cups that is right for getting a beneficial contribution to their health.

Coffee is good for human health. It is up to every man and woman to know the effects of coffee in their bodies and take the right amount of cups so the beneficial effects contribute to their health.

According to an article published in 2010 by Pablo Muriel and Jonathan Arauz[2] from the Department of Pharmacology of Cinvestav - IPN in Mexico, coffee consumption reduces risk of hepatitis and cirrhosis, in addition to counteracting the effects of liver enzymes and hepatocellular carcinoma, the latter being responsible of most liver cancers.

Studies don't focus exclusively on caffeine. Academics[3] from the University of Sidney in Australia, have found that decaffeinated coffee reduces risk of diabetes mellitus type 2. Their analysis was based upon 18 studies with information of 457,922 participants, who reported the association between coffee consumption and diabetes.

In 2002, scientists[4] from the Department of Nutrition of the School of Public Health of Harvard, published a study based upon a cohort of 80,898 women coffee drinkers, who in 1980 were between 34 and 59 years old. After 20 years of following up via questionnaire, only 7,811 women were found having undergone cholecystectomy (surgery to remove the gallbladder). The conclusions of such report indicate that coffee actually has an important role in the prevention of gallstones symptoms among women.

From a meta-analysis based on the search of medical journals between January 1966 and 2008, academics[5] from the Department of Medical Statistics and Epidemiology of the School of Public Health of Sun Yat-sen University in Guangzhou, China, came to conclude that regular and moderate coffee consumption is associated with low risk of getting coronary diseases among women.

Finnish[6] scientists have suggested coffee consumption as a measure to prevent the risk of Parkinson. They came to this hypothesis based on the study of a population of 6,710 men and women between 50 and 79 years old, none of whom had the illness, and by following up over 22 years they observed that people with bigger coffee consumption had littler risk of getting it, though they also noted that this beneficial effect of coffee diminished when accompanied by other factors like smoking, alcohol, little physical activity, body mass, hypertension, among others.

In 2013 an article was published in The World Journal of Biological Psychiatry, which stated that drinking several cups

[2] "Coffee and liver diseases", in Fitoterapia. 2010 Jul;81(5):297-305. doi: 10.1016/j.fitote.2009.10.003.
[3] Huxley R, Lee CM, Barzi F, Timmermeister L, Czernichow S, Perkovic V, Grobbee DE, Batty D, Woodward M., "Coffee, decaffeinated coffee, and tea consumption in relation to incident type 2 diabetes mellitus: a systematic review with meta-analysis", en Arch Intern Med. 2009 Dec 14;169(22):2053-63. doi: 10.1001/archinternmed.2009.439.
[4] Leitzmann MF1, Stampfer MJ, Willett WC, Spiegelman D, Colditz GA, Giovannucci EL., "Coffee intake is associated with lower risk of symptomatic gallstone disease in women", in Gastroenterology. 2002 Dec;123(6):1823-30.
[5] Wu JN1, Ho SC, Zhou C, Ling WH, Chen WQ, Wang CL, Chen YM., "Coffee consumption and risk of coronary heart diseases: a meta-analysis of 21 prospective cohort studies", in Int J Cardiol. 2009 Nov 12;137(3):216-25. doi: 10.1016/j.ijcard.2008.06.051.
[6] Sääksjärvi K, Knekt P, Rissanen H, Laaksonen MA, Reunanen A, Männistö S., "Prospective study of coffee consumption and risk of Parkinson's disease", in Eur J Clin Nutr. 2008 Jul;62(7):908-15.

of coffee in one day reduces risk of suicide both in men and women. So concluded Michel Lucas, researcher at the Department of Nutrition of the School of Public Health of Harvard, when he observed that caffeine, besides stimulating the central nervous system, acts like an antidepressant by boosting the production of some neurotransmitters in the brain, including serotonin, dopamine and norepinephrine, which explains the low risk of depression among drinkers of this infusion.

COFFEE AND HEALTH

It improves alertness, short term memory and it allows a better use of the prefrontal cortex.
Protective effect against degenerative brain diseases such as Alzheimer and Parkinson.

Due to its antioxidants, different studies have linked coffee intake with a reduced risk of skin cancer.

Fights cavities and has anti-inflammatory effects.

Caffeine is chemically similar theophylline, element that helps open airways, commonly used in asthma treatments.

Low risk of coronary disease in women.

Researchers of the Australian Sports Institute found that a single cup of coffee helped athletes give impulse to their muscles and improve their resistance.
It improves performance in athletes.

It prevents gallstones symptoms in women.

It reduces the risk of hepatitis and cirrhosis.

It protects against cancer of colon.

It helps relaxing hyperactive kids.

Decaffeinated coffee reduces the risk of Type 2 diabetes mellitus.

It has antioxidants and antitoxics at cellular level.

Diminishes the risk of depression.
Reduces risk of suicide.

Tradition

Photography:
Francisco J. Pérez Zúñiga

ART AND POPULAR CULTURE IN MEXICO

ART AND POPULAR CULTURE IN MEXICO

José Lozada Tomé, in his essay *"Something About Coffee in the World"*, published in the magazine Arts of Mexico, mentions that there have been times when coffee drinkers have attributed the creation of magnificent works of art to coffee, art created by renowned literature writers, musicians, painters, etc., but there have also been many common people who were cultivators of coffee trees, and others who worked both on plantations, and on the process and trading of coffee beans.

From Colombia, José A. Osorio Lizarazo, published the novel The Harvest, where he describes a coffee-growing population. Manuel Mejía Vallejo, originally from Antioquia, where he was born in 1923, also wrote *At the Foot of the City*. Mario Escobar, in turn, wrote *When the Spirit Passes by on its Own*.

As for poetry, Nicolás Ballona Posada wrote *Coffea Arabica*, whereas Guillermo Edmundo Chávez is the author of *Romance Coffee*, and Ricardo Arango Franco, originally from Caldas, published *Song to the Coffee*.

Nicomedes Santa Cruz, a Peruvian poet wrote with great literary skills the poem *The Coffee*, showing a description of the situation that the black people underwent, first as slaves, then as servants, and later as revolutionaries with the advent of their freedom, but always in allusion to coffee. In the last part, the poem ends as follows:

> I am the same color as you,
> I come from the ground as you,
> Scent and essence we are as one,
> our flavor is sour.
> Come on, brothers, courage,
> the coffee asks of us faith,
> and Changó and Ochúm and Ekué
> claim a clamorous shout
> for our America to be free,
> free like its coffee trees [1]

Another Colombian poet and narrator, Álvaro Mutis, a Mexico resident for many years, resorts to the sight of a coffee plantation to convey the magic and the forces of nature, in his poem *Nocturnal*.

Cassiano Ricardo, a Brazilian poet, wrote *Young Woman Drinking Coffee*, describing a brief and intense journey from a bar in Paris, where a young woman is drinking coffee. He has no idea how the coffee has arrived there across the ocean and the blue sky above, by boat and by train, in addition to overcoming any other hindrances whatsoever. He also wonders how, despite the grower's weariness and the damages caused by nature in his plantation, the grower has thrived on all these vicissitudes and grown the coffee successfully.

In Mexico, he was also popularly inspired to sing to the coffee, as well as to mention it in lyrics to children's songs, such as *Little Threads of Gold, or One, Two, Three* or in satirical verses like the Calaveras by José Guadalupe Posada, not to mention the crowd-pleasing stanzas about the regions where coffee is grown, like in *To Coatepec, that is My Land, by María Enriqueta* (1912), or in the songs *Cafeto and Envío*, which are well-known in Huatusco, Veracruz. The well renowned composer, Agustín Lara was also inspired to compose *Flowers of Coffee Plantations*, using these metaphors:

> Flowers of coffee are in your mouth,
> scent of flowers, it makes me sigh;
> feathers of cardinals, lovely flowers,
> flowers of coffee, I found in your mouth.
> And like flowers of coffee it smelled,
> I dare say something, I kissed its surroundings;
> And then that tasty flavor in your mouth,
> in that kiss of love, left me spellbound! [2]

[1] Cited by Pérez Pérez, Juan Ramón and Salvador Díaz Cárdenas..
[2] Cited by Pérez Pérez, Juan Ramón and Salvador Díaz Cárdenas, p 81-84.

The Mexican writers that mention the aroma of coffee are, amongst others, Jaime Sabines, who writes "It is good to drink coffee when it is cold", as well as Oscar Oliva, Manuel Gutiérrez Nájera and Ricardo Pozas.[3] Rosario Castellanos dedicated her poem *Coffee plantations of Chiapas* to the growing of coffee:

Coffee pickers in the Soconusco.
Luxury stands out in the yard,
so much deliciousness around
(Stripped coffee tree,
look down and smile)
With one hand they choose
the better beans,
with the other hand they throw away,
they measure and evaluate.
Wisdom goes around in rough dresses.
Let me take the right steps,
wisely like theirs.[4]

[3] Bartra Vergés, Armando, cit. p. 40.
[4] *Ibidem*, p. 80.

Inspired by the form of the poem *El Cenzontle*, written by King Nezahualcoyotl, Fausto Cantú Peña, while being General Director of the Mexican Institute of Coffee, wrote the poem *A Whole Universe in a Bean:*

I love the trill of the singing birds
and the polychromy of playful butterflies,
the tonality of green jade covering
the rainforest tropic.
I love the incandescent white color of its flowers,
the cherry red of the sweet berries,
the golden seed kept in the wise parchment,
the seductive aroma of roasting over live fire.
The transparency of the enervating liquor
poured into the mug, the Talavera (ceramics from the city
of Puebla),or the fine porcelain.
I love the stimulating beverage of creative imagination,
but what I love the most is my mother, Earth, the Sun,
giver of life, the rain that makes Nature fruitful,
men, women and children who cultivate the tree
who give us the fruit of coffee,
which makes us "toast" to friendship and the peace
of the nation…and the world.

In music, back in 1732, even Johann Sebastian Bach composed "The Coffee Cantata", where he refers to a great liking for the drink, especially from women –grandmother, mother, and daughter.

Coffee has also been an inspiration in popular music. Compound pieces of music proliferate in several rhythms, such as the Montuno son *Coffee*, the danzón *Ay Mamá Iné*, and others like *Grinding coffee, Café-Café, Ojalá que Llueva Café*, to name just a few.

In regard to theater, in 1750 Carlos Goldoni first showed the three-act comedy play *La Bottega del Caffè*, its protagonists being a coffee store and one of its habitual customers, Don Marzio. And in more recent times, television has also been inspired likewise by the valuable coffee bean. For example, in the Colombian soap opera *Café con aroma de mujer* (Coffee with aroma of woman), which has been most famous in the whole of Latin America.

Painters, engravers and muralists refer to the subject, as well: Vincent Van Gogh made the painting named *The Night Café* as "the place where one can be ruined, go crazy and commit crimes" as stated by the great painter.

Moreover, there are works of art like the painting by J. Villa, named the *Allegory of the Coffee*, which has decorated Costa Rica's National Theater ever since the turn of the 19th century. Other artistic creations include *The History of Coffee, Chronicle of Caldas, Goodbye to Coffee* by the Colombian Alipio Jaramillo, Gonzalo Ariza and Eduardo Ramírez Castro; the wall painting *the Coffee*, by the Brazilian Cándido Portinari; as well as the collection Coffee 1, 2, 3, 4 y 5, by the Mexican painter and engraver, Francisco Toledo.

In terms of philately, there are numerous stamps from many countries. The work of important artists is shown by these stamps, with images of plantations on them, as well as coffee cultivators, plants, beans, tools for the preparation of the drink, the steaming coffee, etc.

There are also acrostics, verses and other expressions regarding coffee. For instance, the acrostic of Perrin completed by Armando Fuentes.

Hot: It warms up body and soul
Sour: Without the foreign presence of sugar or any strange liquids
Strong: Concentrated essence, neither diluted nor distorted
Scarce: If there is too little of it, it must be good.. [5]

A Talleyrand, a prominent French politician and diplomat of the late 18th and early 19th century, liked coffee, which he described as follows:

Hot as hell,
Black as coal,
Strong as the devil,
Sweet as love. [6]

The Grand Inquisitor of Europe, the Austrian Chancellor Clemens Lothar Metternich, said that coffee should be: hot like love, sweet as sin and black as hell.

Other sayings that are full of wisdom point out:

Coffee boiled, coffee spoiled.

Nothing worse than loving someone for the second time and drinking reheated coffee.

Coffee is drunk without sugar. If it is good, you do not need it, if it is bad, not worth drinking.

It might be said that the Mexican expression "Estar café" (being like sour coffee) can be used to express a big tantrum.

[5] Confederación Mexicana de Productores de Café, *100% Café*, México, DF, s/f, p. 15, cited by Pérez Pérez, Juan Ramón and Salvador Díaz Cárdenas, *op. cit*, pág. 102.
[6] Vilhena de Toledo, Vera and Cándida Vilares Gancho, *Sua Majestade o café*, Modern Editor, 1972, Brazil, p. 5, cited in *ibidem*. Rosa Carreño, in her book *Lectura del Café. Guía práctica*, reproduces a very similar sentence: "Coffee must be / black as hell, / strong as death / and sweet as love…" citing it as a "Turkish proverb"..

Other artistic manifestations occur through traditions and popular beliefs.

One is the traditional celebration named "The Widow", held in several towns where coffee is cultivated, like Córdoba, Veracruz. Here, laborers build a cross and place it upon a tree on a farm decorated with flowers and bright-colored paper, which is something eye-catching. Also, they make necklaces with ripe coffee fruits and a cane for the owners of the farm on the day of the celebration, as a symbol of authority. The workers are treated to a meal, where tamales, barbecued chicken and mole are served, and they drink beer and even firewater.

As well as in the celebrations of corn, before coffee reached Mexico, there is a contest to name the queen of coffee. On the day of the ceremony, she dresses in white, representing the flower of coffee. Another young woman dresses in green, representing the tender fruit, and then another woman wears a red dress, representing a ripe cherry. Last, "the widow", dresses in black.

There is also a famous coffee fair held in Cuetzalan, Puebla, on October 4. Even though it coincides with the feast of the patron saint of the town San Francisco, it is more of an indigenous than a Catholic celebration. Valdiosera narrates it this way:

> "The cuetzaltecos express themselves as they are on the week of October 4, through the Spell of the Coffee Fair. Women dress in the style of their old grandmothers from the Totonaco Nahua people, their hairstyle with purple and blue laces, their hair is intertwined to create a headdress. The men are at the head of the procession in albo pants. On this day the crop yield is celebrated".[7]

An effort made in the early 1970s, at the initiative of Maria Felicitas Garza Cantú, was the impetus to handicrafts made from coffee plants. This was registered by Lulú Vargas Villa de Lee, who describes wooden coffee crafts since the end of 1974. The old trees, traditionally used as firewood, she states, have been exploited to develop carvings. At first pens, cups, sculptures, were made, then dishes, rustic tables, lighters, pins,

[7] Valdiosera. "La feria del café, Cuetzalan, Puebla, 4 de octubre", in *Artes de México*, núm. 192, year XXII, El café en México, 1978, p. 45.

necklaces strung with beads made from coffee beans. They later made covers for chairs and even fine folding screens, in openwork detail that make them very appreciated. [8]

At the initiative of the Commission for the Promotion and Development of the Chiapas Coffee, in 2008 began the rescue and repairs of a building built in 1913, in the city of Tuxtla Gutierrez. It was Dr. Rafael Ramos Grajales' homeroom, which he donated to the State Government before dying. After being a regional museum and headquarters of peasant organizations, in 2011 it was established as the Coffee Museum, and was in charge of the State Council on Culture and Arts of Chiapas. At present, this museum offers guided tours for people to know about the origin and history of coffee, its roots and evolution in Chiapas, in addition to illustrating the processes involved in both its transformation and trading. It also has a tiny tree nursery, a tasting laboratory, a barista and a room for temporary exhibitions. Workshops and cultural activities taking place in this room are intended to strengthen the differentiation and positioning of the Chiapas coffee quality in domestic and foreign markets. This increases domestic consumption. In addition, other museums were built, which you will find in the electronic version of this book and in the encyclopedic dictionary.

[8] Lulú Vargas Villa de Lee. "Café: una artesanía nueva", in *Artes de México*, #. 192, year XXII, El café en México, 1978, pp. 61-62.

Coffee and Art

Lithography of V. de Munguía and sons, History of a grain of coffee, included in
La Ciencia Recreativa. Agricultura e Industria l, D. José Joaquín Arriaga.

Mural under the direction of Teodoro Caño. Crafts School founded by María Felícitas Cantú de Cantú. Coatepec, Ver.

Collective Mural made under the Inmecafé Program Coffee and Art 1976 Garnica, Jalapa Ver.

Ángel Zárraga
La merienda de dos niñas
1916
Oil on canvas
78 x 63
Private collection

Diego Rivera
La terrace du café
1915
Oil on canvas
78 x 63
The Metropolitan Museum of Art, N.Y. Collection

José María Estrada
Taza
1830
Oil/plate
Roberto Montenegro collection

Johann Morizt Rugendas
La plaza mayor de Córdoba con el ayuntamiento, los portales y la parroquia
c. 1831
Oil on canvas
Museo Nacional de HIstoria collection

Diego Rivera
Naturaleza Muerta
1918
Pencil/paper
24 x 31.3
The Art Museum of Chicago collection

Ramón Alva de la Canal
Café de nadie
1924
Oil and collage on canvas
78 x 64
MUNAL

Manuel Manilla
(El café del conejo)
c. 1890
Lead engraving
A. Vargas Arroyo collection

Cafeto
Fausto Cantú Cantú
1991
Dry-point engraving
22 x 25

Fermín Revueltas
El café de 5 centavos
1925
Watercolor/ paper
33 x 29
Blanca Maples Arce collection

Caffea
Fausto Cantú Cantú
1991
Dry-point engraving
13 x 13

Jorge González Camarena
El café
1932
(Illustration taken from Revista de Revistas, February 14, 1932, p.29)

Fermín Revueltas
La cosechadora de Café
c.1925
Ink/ paper
20.5 x 29
Blanca Maples Arce collection

Frida Kahlo
Apuntes para Pancho Villa y la Adelita
ca. 1926, Pencil/ paper
21 x 28

Rufino Tamayo
La Cafetera
1960
Oil on canvas
135 x 195
Bernard Lewin collection

José Clemente Orozco
Café
c. 1994
Gouache/ paper
40.7 x 58.5
Daniel Goldberg collection

Luis López Loza
Cafetera
1973
Engraving
34.5 x 23.5
Arnaldo Coen collection

Ramón Alva de la Canal
Maples Arce en el Café de nadie
1924 - 1925
Pencil/ paper
45 x 29
Blanca de Maples Arce collection

José Luis Romo
Novenario del 6 de julio
1988
Mixed media/ paper
67 x 85
López Quiroga Gallery collection

Arnaldo Coen
Cafetera y molino
1988
Pencil/ paper
33 x 85.5
Private collection

Francisco Toledo
El goloso de Guelatao
1985
Mixed media/ fossil
(From the series Lo que el viento a Juárez)
Private collection

Arnaldo Coen
Francisco Toledo
Café num 3
1988
Ink/ paper
36.6 x 50.3
Private collection

Richard Zela
Coffee ink on paper

Richard Zela
Coffee ink on paper

Modernity

CURRENT COFFEE CONSUMPTION

CURRENT COFFEE CONSUMPTION

Domestic consumption has increased by 35% over the last decade. There are more and more places where you can drink coffee in new varieties, causing a change in the habits of Mexicans. Teenagers and young people drink it more than they used to, due to the market entry of new coffee shops. And the myth about the damage to health is dying out. The perception of local consumption has improved.

The availability of roasted grain in retail is very limited, but over the last ten years it has increased by 20.4 percentage points on an annual basis. The growth of the chains of stores specialized in brewing has created opportunities for retail sale of ground coffee. People want to drink better quality coffee at home. This is demonstrated by a sustained growth of 10.3% in this type of selling on an annual average, since 2005.[1]

The demand for soluble coffee is very high in volume, but has experienced a decline in its market share. A decade ago,

it accounted for 88.7% of the volume of retail, although 83.6 percentage points are estimated for 2015.

Annual growth rates in the purchase of grain toasted by gastronomic operators, has meant that aromatic ground coffee amounts to half the consumption in restaurants.

According to estimates for 2015, the per capita consumption in Mexico will be 1.85 kg. This indicator is ten times lower than the consumption of Finland, the country with the highest per capita consumption. In Latin American countries similar to ours, such as Colombia or Costa Rica, this type of consumption is doubled, while in Brazil it is tripled. Market campaigns aimed at increasing the drinking of Mexican coffee, along with the growth of establishments offering a wide variety of brewed drinks and better informed and more demanding consumers, drive the market.

Why do we drink coffee? A more intriguing question would be why you are reading this book. In life, we have many interests. Some of them have to do with our work, whereas others are related to our lifestyle, and sometimes there happens to be a combination between them. Coffee, as a consumer product, is driven by different motivations. Just as there are varieties of coffee trees, there are also different types of consumers. Humans seek to establish categories to understand the world and to transform it. There are several marketing strategies to foster the demand for a product, one of them being to determine consumer segmentation. By identifying customers accurately, bidders might direct their efforts to please their tastes and therefore there will be a demand increase.

Today, in Mexico, there are five types of consumers pinpointed:[2] Heritage and practicality, they drink coffee as a custom inherited at home, seeking practicality in consuming; Conscious pleasure, they enjoy the drink, they know how to find good coffee without being experts on the subject;

---

[1] Euromonitor International, "Análisis del mercado nacional y regional del café en México", September 2012.

Stamina and speed, it is part of breakfast, they need it to wake up; Self-indulgence and socialization: their aim is to taste and mix flavors, coffee lets them share moments with friends; Belonging and satisfaction: they enjoy the adventure of drinking coffee and its relationship with the context in question, in search of a full experience.

Based on consumer surveys, it is known that the highest percentages of types of coffee that people drink more is the Caffe Americano (between 35 and 45% depending on the profile), followed by decaffeinated coffee (30%), mainly consumed by the second consumer type, namely, *Conscious pleasure*. The people who drink more cups of coffee a day (3-6 cups) are those described in type four –belonging and satisfaction, apart from being the biggest spenders on a monthly average on consumption at and outside the home. Although, as expected, below them are consumers of the self-indulgence and socialization type, despite their low consumption of cups (3-4 coffees a week), obviously outside the home. To complete these data, it should be stated that people who spend less on coffee are those of the stamina and speed type, as they buy soluble coffee at supermarkets. Nevertheless, this profile represents the largest type of sales in coffee consumption in Mexico. This turns out to be paradoxical if the motivations of these consumers are observed, which gives little importance to the quality of the drink, its main concern being its quick preparation. The conclusions from these surveys suggest that the increased

demand for coffee is down to the fact of the drink being at hand, and most consumers have the perception that good coffee is hard to come by.

Recommendations for consumption growth, in this sense, are promotion campaigns to extend the polarized scenario of large consumers, who generally only distinguish soluble coffee and coffee made in coffee-makers. It is desirable that people know about the wide variety of ways to prepare the drink, in order to put an end to the myth that good coffee is an inaccessible luxury.

Currently, SAGARPA is displaying the campaign "Have Mexican Coffe" aiming to re-launch and increase the consumption of the mexican aromatic both domestic and abroad.

[2] The Association, "Segmentación de consumidores de café", Mexico, 2014.

SPECIALTY COFFEES

SPECIALTY COFFEES

The first time the term specialty coffee was used was back in 1974, in the American publication Tea and Coffee Trade Journal, International Perspective on Coffee and Tea Industries since 1901, as the slogan says. The author of the article, Erna Knutsen, used it to describe better tasting beans that were produced in special microclimates.

At present, to establish a coffee specialty, the international cupping form is used, developed by the Committee on Technical Standards of the Specialty Coffee Association of America, created in 1982 by a group of professionals whose common interest was to discuss and determine the standardized features of specialty coffees.

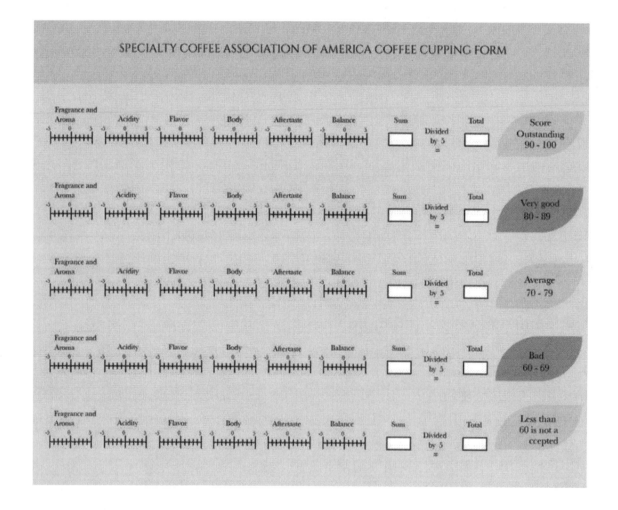

This form is a scoring system that assesses five stages in the process of coffee tasting: fragrance, aroma, taste, feeling and body. The form contains six areas of assessment, namely, fragrance and aroma, acidity, flavor, body, aftertaste and balance, and the first five areas are scored from 0 to 10. But in the balance area, there is a score of -5 to +5, where the taster provides a general score based on the combination of all the aspects of coffee. The sum of all the scoring points is divided into five, with a total result on a decimal scale. It is estimated that coffee scored from 9.0 to 10.0 is exceptional, from 8.0 to 8.9, good-tasting, from 7.0 to 7.9, it is considered as a commercial average quality coffee, from 6.0 to 6.9 it is poor quality coffee, and last, below six points, it is judged to be defective.

In order for a certain coffee to be classified as specialty, it should exceed eight scoring points. Tasters who help producers to assess the quality of their beans are responsible for carrying out this assessment.

In 2004, the Mexican Association of Specialty Coffee Shops was established. Its aim is to "open new niches in the domestic market and to increase domestic consumption, based on the quality through all stages, from seed to cup".

Specialty coffees represent a great opportunity to increase profits for producers, since its differentiation from conventional coffee breaks barriers in international prices for certain commodities. It stands to reason that this distinction is not achieved overnight and requires the collaboration of each and every stakeholder in the process of coffee, plus a plan that considers their ongoing training. In Mexico, conditions are ripe to promote this production; although its percentage is low, there are notable examples in Chiapas, Veracruz, Oaxaca, Puebla and Hidalgo.

Organic Coffee

The cultivation of organic coffee began in 1963 at the Finca Irlanda, a coffee plantation in Tapachula, Chiapas, and got the first international certification in 1967. At that farm, they focused on "implementing organic and biodynamic agriculture in their crops. Organic cultivation involves not using chemicals in fertilization processes and pest control, as well as making biodynamic compost and other preparations to stimulate the life of both the soil and plants".[1] Even though it was consolidated by the end of the 1980s, in the middle of the coffee crisis, in the period of 2007/2008, coffee was cultivated in 176,105.70 hectares, i.e., 22.43% of all the hectares with coffee grown in Mexico. In 2005, it was estimated that organic coffee was produced in more than 145 municipalities and 1,250 communities, "characterized by smallholding farmers and, in most cases, by indigenous people who had organized themselves to differentiate their products, and thus looking to get more added value".[2]

Organic agriculture is a production system that uses of natural inputs, maximizes nutrient recycling and avoids the use of products derived from fossil fuels such as chemical fertilizers and pesticides. Through this system, any toxic waste

[1] Pérez Poumián, Magda Leticia, "La finca Irlanda: Modelo organizacional de la agricultura orgánica-biodinámica, sustentable y responsable. Cambio y estrategia en una organización cafetalera en el Soconusco, 1960-2006", doctoral thesis on Organizational studies, UAM Iztapalapa, México, 2006.
[2] Escamilla et al. (2005) by López López, Édgar y Caamal Cauich, "Los costos de producción del café orgánico del estado de Chiapas y el precio justo en el mercado internacional", in *Revista Mexicana de Economía Agrícola y de los Recursos Naturales*, vol. 2, #1, México, 2009, p. 179.

is prevented not only in the product but in transportation, packing, packaging and labeling.[3]

Through the convergence of modern cultivation processes and traditional ones, passed down through generations, small farmers seek a balance between acceptable profitability and the application of models to prevent natural resources from being harmed. Also, by conforming to the rules imposed on producers by the market, they struggle to have their own brand and certificate of origin.

Thus, small farmers and their organizations, particularly in Chiapas, have resorted to exchanges and negotiations with companies and international organizations.

In selecting coffee beans of export quality, youths play their part in their communities. They sit by the sides of a machine

and its moving web on which the grain has already been selected; here the grain is less blurred and they inspect it by looking at it while scattering it skillfully with their hands. It is almost a grain by grain quality control.

Before reaching the fine manual selection process, the shell has been removed, and the selector has done its part by size and weight in three categories: European, American and domestic consumption. Only premium quality grains pass through the final selection process.

An experience in the production of organic coffee is the Biosphere Reserve "El Triunfo", in Chiapas. It is a reserve that as well as being one of the most important and bio diverse in the world, is the birthplace of the famous Shade Grown Mexico. Farmers have developed techniques to harvest coffee of the highest quality, certified as eco-friendly,

[3] Instituto Nacional de Capacitación del Sector Agropecuario, A. C. (INCA Rural)/Consejo Mexicano del Café, *Manual para la Cafeticultura Mexicana, Cuaderno 5, Cultivo Orgánico del Cafeto*, México, 1997.

since its cultivation involves minimal impact on the fragile and valuable environment of its location.

Since the program was introduced in 1998, coffee plantations kept as rainforests had a 220% increase and coffee exports rose by 50%, compared with former years. It has also succeeded in ensuring that farmers involved in the program get a higher price than that in the domestic market, which at times has become 60% above its listing price.[4]

In organic coffee plantations, farmers conserve the soil and fertility through natural fertilizers produced from natural pulp of coffee and cattle manure generated within the same farm area.

According to some scholars,[5] organic coffee "could be considered as a measure to protect the income of producers from the global uncertainty of market prices. Under this production system, besides seeking to get a higher price for their product, producers take part in a strategy of sustainable agriculture, avoiding the irrational exploitation of the land, which would ensure their permanence in time".

From this standpoint, sustainability means not only preserving nature but also seeking economic stability for producers and, consequently, for their families and the society that they are immersed in. The term sustainable coffee was adopted by the International Coffee Organization (ICO) in the first decade of the 21st century as a result of analyzed statistics during the

[4] *Nuestro Café. Un viaje a la Biósfera El Triunfo en Chiapas y a los sueños de las comunidades que cultivan nuestro café*. Café Sirena, S. de R.L. de C.V., 2007, México.
[5] Delgado Juárez, Gabriel y Pablo Pérez Akaki, "Evaluación de la conversión a café orgánico usando la metodología de opciones reales", in *Contaduría y Administración*, vol. 58, núm. 1, UNAM, México, 2003.

last quarter of the 20th century. The data showed a steady increase in production, which caused two negative effects: the overexploitation of farmland and a decline in prices that could not be controlled due to the breakdown of the quota system in 1989.

In February, 2013, the International Center for Tropical Agriculture estimated that by 2050 there would be a reconversion of the best areas for coffee. They would rise from 600 to 850-900 meters above sea level and there would be a loss of 35.6% in areas suitable for growing coffee if we do not take action now to counteract the looming adversity.[6]

Amongst adaptation practices are these scenarios:[7]

Organic coffee production generates many benefits, the most important are the conservation of biodiversity and economic sustainability of producers. This distinction, however, is

Also, mitigation practices can be the following:

Having crops with diversified shade.

An integrated shade management.

Renewing coffee varieties resistant to high temperatures, droughts, pests and diseases.

Setting up micro-irrigation systems and rain water harvesting.

Making use of solar dryers.

Reforesting en bloc on a small scale.

Protecting water sources, like streams and creeks.

Also, mitigation practices can be the following:

Shade maintenance.

Maintenance of coffee trees.

Retrofitting degraded areas into agroforestry systems with and without coffee.

Preserving and enriching the soil with organic matter.

Reusing and recycling waste from the production of biogas with honey water.

Reducing the slash-and-burn practice.

Reducing or avoiding the extraction of fuel wood.

Implementing low-emission and efficient technology for coffee processing (pulping, screening, fermentation).

Diversifying production.

Seeking to improve the availability of credit resources, training and technical assistance.

Strengthening the organization of producers.

more popular in the US and European markets where consumers seek fair trade, in addition to the certification of organic coffee. Mexico was the first country to export with this double certification. Its production is currently concentrated in Chiapas, Oaxaca, Veracruz and Puebla, but could be extended to other states with success, thanks to global demand and the gradual growth that has been proven in the market. The importance of coffee in Mexico is widely recognized by academic and agricultural officials, who have made promotion efforts in society, hoping to boost domestic consumption growth.

[6] Projections exposed by Mónica G. Morales, Conservación Internacional, at Convención Internacional del Café, held on July 3 to 5, 2015 in Mexico City.
[7] Proposals presented in Tuxtla Gutiérrez, Chiapas, in Foro Estatal "Vulnerabilidad, Adaptación y Mitigación del sector cafetalero ante el cambio climático" (junio 2011), whose organization committee was constituted by: Secretaría de Medio Ambiente e Historial Natural (SEMAHN), Comisión para el Desarrollo y Fomento del Café de Chiapas (COMCAFÉ), Comisión Nacional de Áreas Naturales Protegidas (CONANP) – Reservas La Sepultura y El Triunfo, Federación Indígena Ecológica de Chiapas, S.S.S. (FIECH), Programa de las Naciones Unidas para el Desarrollo en México -Manejo de Riesgos y Desastres en el Estado de Chiapas (PNUD), El Colegio de la Frontera Sur (ECOSUR), Promotores de Alternativas Tecnológicas para la Producción Orgánica, S.C. (PATPO) y Conservation International Mexico, A.C. (CI).

TASTERS AND BARISTAS

TASTERS AND BARISTAS

Tasters

According to the Manifesto of the Coffee Taster,[1] the experience of tasting consists of the following parts:

1. Finding faults.
2. Looking for pleasant flavors.
3. Recognizing a familiar taste.
4. Evaluating identity.
5. Determining if the quality of the coffee is poor, fair, average, good, very good or outstanding.
6. Noticing the results.

An experienced taster must recognize the processes involved all the way from seed to cup, so prior knowledge of the process of transformation is necessary. Precisely, these data will determine the valuation of a specialty coffee and its future value.

Among the features listed in the manifesto, the assessor must have a good memory, he needs to remember the quality in the cup of coffee from many regions, be a lover of details, save the information collected per year and embark on a commitment to sharing this information with producers, among others.

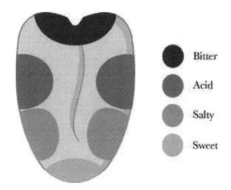

Bitter
Acid
Salty
Sweet

Barista

The word "barista" is of Italian origin and refers to a person who works in a bar, either the owner or the manager responsible for preparing drinks. It was incorporated to the English language as a foreign word in order to refer to a person who specializes in making drinks based on espresso-type coffee. Specifically, the United States was the country where the promotion of this activity began in the 1980s.

In regard to the espresso coffee machine, its inventor was the Italian Luigio Bezzera, who patented it in 1901 and displayed it at the International Fair of Milan in 1906. This event is important if we take a look at the background suggested by the very same associations of baristas. We would have to wait over 70 years to see the changes proposed for this drink. In Spanish, the word barista was included and remained unchanged and its meaning was attributed to the Anglo-Saxons.

[1] Katzeff, Paul, *El Manifiesto de los catadores de café*, Thanksgiving Coffee Company, EUA, 2001.

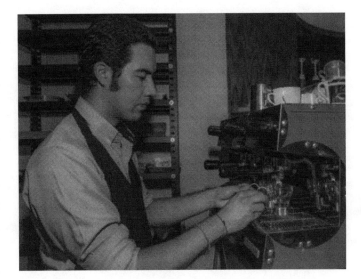

It is now considered that a barista is a theoretical and practical professional in the art of preparing drinks with high quality coffee. His theoretical knowledge must allow him to differentiate the varieties of grains and recognize their characteristics, besides knowing which type of roast and ground coffee is the most suitable for different preparations and he must also distinguish which other drinks mixed with coffee, delight the palate. On the practical level, all this knowledge must be demonstrated, hence the boom of baristas competitions.

Baristas are also known as coffee sommeliers and some language purists want the word "cafetista" (coffeeist) to be used in the Spanish language, instead. There is no doubt that the word might change according to acceptance or social rejection. Whatever the word might be, we will know that this person is a meticulous coffee lover.

HOW TO DRINK COFFEE

HOW TO DRINK COFFEE[1]

Regions and countries have adopted various preparation methods and habits according to their culture and customs. There are places where people drink to cool off or due to the stimulating properties. Some others drink it for its taste and flavor and prepare it as a stronger drink.

The drink that we call coffee is an infusion or decoction of coffee beans ground in water. The water extracts all the flavor and fragrance from the grain. This principle has not changed since coffee drinking became a habit, but what has changed is the elements required to prepare the infusion.

The first important element is water, if it comes from the tap, it has been treated with chlorine and its derivatives for disinfection, therefore, it needs boiling for five minutes before using it. Another option is the mineral waters of neutral flavor, which regardless of brand, provide the best option for preparing the drink. To make coffee, the water should not be at boiling point, yet very hot, the ideal temperature being between 85 and 96° C. You can also get a coffee infusion with cold water, which must be very concentrated and left to stand for ten hours to then obtain a good quality drink by adding hot water.

The second element is the coffee-maker or coffee machine. According to its system, it can be gravity, which reproduces the traditional method of pouring hot water into a filter containing ground coffee and below is the cup that the infusion falls into, and through air-driven water, it rises and is placed above the filter on which the ground coffee is located. Then when the water goes down, it makes way for the infusion, and through vapor pressure, the water quickly runs through the ground coffee.

The third essential element is coffee itself. At present, you can purchase innumerable mixtures, all of them combined to

produce good-body coffee, a feeling of strength and fullness of flavor that fills the mouth when it has been retained for a moment; acidity, which causes a slight stinging sensation or a slightly acidic taste and aroma, basically action from the essences of the grain itself on the palate.

Trying different types of coffee and even preparing it in the traditional way and in different coffee machines will help us know about many variations and flavor characteristics. It is advisable to try until we find the type of coffee and the way to prepare it that we like it best. As said about happiness, the important thing is not to find it, but to enjoy the journey we are on while seeking it.

[1] These suggestions and recommendations have been taken mainly from the following writings: Ilario, José (editor), *La guía Epicur del café, copa y puro*, Barcelona, Epicur Publicaciones, s/f; Instituto Mexicano del Café. *Secretos del café*, México, 1966; Hernández, Avelino, *La cultura de tomar café. Guía para estimular el gusto por el buen café*, México, Mexican Confederation of Coffee Producers, s/f; Pérez Pérez, Juan Ramón and Salvador Díaz Cárdenas, *El Café, bebida que conquistó al mundo*, México, Universidad Autónoma Chapingo, 2000, and Carreño, Rosa, Lectura del café. Guía práctica, México, Selector, 2002.

EXPERTS' RECOMMENDATIONS FOR PREPARING THE DRINK ARE

Ensuring the freshness of coffee, buying it weekly -grain natural oils are volatile and once roasted and ground, coffee aroma and body decrease. If you have roasted and ground beans, it is recommended that you consume your coffee in seven days, but if you want to keep it longer, it is advisable to store the unground roasted grain.

Selecting evenly toasted grains, the color should be even; avoid marbled or speckled grains.

A preference for medium roast. Oils volatilize more rapidly with more intense roasting.

Buying coffee from high altitude areas. This information, if true, confirms origin and quality and is more important than the name of the region.

Keeping the roasted and ground coffee beans in a tightly closed container in a cool, dry atmosphere (the refrigerator is a good choice), otherwise taste deteriorates if exposed to air or to scented products.

Water is important. For best results, use pure water. Water with chlorine taste affects the quality of the drink.

Keep your coffee-maker perfectly clean. Before use, rinse with hot water. After each use, wash it carefully without using soap or detergent; rinse with hot water and dry it.

It is best to use the full capacity of your coffee maker. To prepare less coffee, use a smaller coffee maker. Under no circumstances should you use less than two thirds of the full capacity of the coffee maker.

Time is important. Carefully follow the instructions regarding the time for coffee making. Consider that the degree of coffee grind (fine, medium, coarse) is related to the time that it will have contact with the water during preparation. The less time the water is in contact with the coffee, the finer the ground must be. If the grain is very thick and water or steam passes through it too quickly, the infusion will be too light, tasteless and with very little aroma.

Paper filters should be stored away from pungent-smelling food, so that they do not absorb scents that the coffee would get.

For best results put an average measure of two tablespoons, or its equivalent to medium-sized coffee grounds, for every cup of water.

The coffee should never boil. When the coffee boils, it acquires an unpleasant taste.

Serve the coffee immediately after preparation. Fresh coffee tastes better. If you cannot serve it immediately, place your coffee pot in a bowl of hot water (in a double boiler) or on a very slow heat to keep the temperature at which it should be served.

Coffee should be served immediately after it has been prepared, it is best to serve it in porcelain cups of coffee. This does not add any undesirable taste and retains heat better than any other material.

Coffee should be drunk at its maximum endurable temperature.

GASTRONOMY

GASTRONOMY

Gastronomy involves studying the relationship between man and his food. Chefs are not only responsible for developing recipes; in addition they have a great talent for research. They gather information about products, methods of preparation, tastes and culinary possibilities. Chefs experience time after time until they get the accurate taste, the right consistency, and the required cooking.

Their connection with coffee has become increasingly closer. As taste lovers, they have been great amateur drinkers, but have also included, especially in confectionery, essences or extracts derived from the drink. And as days go by, they discover new ways to combine food and coffee. For example,

in pairings, the interest in specialty coffees and the outstanding reviews have highlighted the relation of coffee to the flavors of food. Also, certain recipes have been proposed, which consist of marinated fish with coffee and recently, besides roasted coffee, they have experimented with green beans.

Research leads to innovation and, thus, the Basque chef Josean Alija, promotes the infusion of green coffee with pea sprout, the roasting of green coffee in the kitchen of the restaurant and its infusion with mushroom broth with additional aromas from dried fruits. To encourage culinary creativity, we must add another formula: "Black beer coffee, made from a base of different roasts of coffee".

Café de olla

The origin of *café de olla* (literally pot coffee) has not been determined accurately. One legend suggests that during the Mexican revolution in the early 20th century, the "camp followers" prepared it to make their soldiers feel strong. To the coffee-based drink they added cinnamon sticks, cloves, and they used brown sugar as a sweetener. Furthermore, chocolate was added as an energizer.

This recipe is prepared with some variations in different regions of Mexico. This coffee is usual at breakfast, accompanied with sweet bread, after lunch and at dinner. In several taverns and restaurants throughout the country, when you order a cup of coffee, you get a steaming clay cup whose handle you hold with one hand and whose edge you hold with the other. This raises a smile on the diner's face that is concealed in the first sip, but the smile appears again during tasting.

On national holidays, people have it with churros, donuts, *"pambazos"* (Mexican dish), *"memelas"* (Mexican tortillas) and many other dishes of our cuisine.

In rural and urban populations, it is common for families and friends to have it when they gather to mitigate the pain from the loss of a loved one. During the celebrations of the Day of the Dead, a pot is laid graveside while people share food and stories of the deceased for the whole night. Undoubtedly, it is an element of our national identity renewed day by day with habit and tradition.

According to Juan Ramon Pérez y Pérez and Salvador Díaz Cárdenas, this is the recipe:
Boil water for two or three minutes with brown sugar to taste in a clay pot, adding some cinnamon sticks. Remove it from the heat and add two tablespoons of coffee per cup of water. Stir well and cover the pan. Leave it to stand for five minutes and serve it in clay pots. In some regions, it is prepared without cinnamon.

RECIPES

RECIPES

DRINKS AND COCKTAILS

Coffee preparation has a wide range of possibilities, even more so when applied to confectionery and beverage processing. The following recipes are usual mainly in Mexico and Latin America, with ingredients that originated in our country and the above-mentioned regions, or are widely consumed at least in this area. But let us start off by describing how it was prepared many years ago...

Mayan Coffee

Place a kilo (2.20 lbs) of velvet coffee on a skillet and toast on low heat, stirring constantly to prevent sticking. Remove when the beans turn black. In the same skillet, roast a teaspoon of aniseed, twelve cinnamon sticks and five grams of tabasco pepper, for twenty minutes. Grind the coffee slowly and start adding the toasted spices. When everything is ground, store and use it to prepare your black coffee. This preparation is also used as medicine: take a handful of this coffee with a few feverfew leaves, add some cattle fat and put the mixture on the chest and forehead to lower the temperature. (P)[2]

Mexican Coffee

It spills 120 ml. of warm coffee newly done in a cup. He adds 30 ml. of liquor of coffee and 30 ml. of tequila. It covers with well-trodden cream and dusts cinnamon and cocoa in powder.

Coffee of pot

Boil water with brown sugar (piloncillo) for 2 to 3 minutes in a clay pot, add cinnamon sticks, remove from fire and add 2 tablespoons of coffee for each cup of water. Stir well and cover the pot. Let it sit for 5 minutes and serve in small clay jugs. In some regions this type of coffee is prepared without cinnamon. (I)

---

[1] This letter is used to identify the recipes taken from *Recetario del café*. Consejo Nacional para la Cultura y las Artes. Culturas Populares, México, 1997, 136 pp.
[2] This letter is used to identify the recipes taken from Pérez Pérez, Juan Ramón and Salvador Díaz Cárdenas, op. cit.

Exquisite Coffee with Milk

Boil a teaspoon of ground coffee in about ¼ liter of milk for fifteen minutes. Then add one or two eighths of an ounce of isinglass (isinglass: gelatin made from the skins and offal from fish; it can be replaced with common gelatin). Let it boil for a few minutes and retrieve from fire. Sweeten with good sugar. Mexican cuisine, 19th century. (R)

Refreshment El Cafetal

Put crushed ice in a cold cup of American coffee, add two tablespoons of cold concentrated chocolate and stir a bit. Serve in tall glasses, add whipped or Chantilly cream, and garnish with a syrup cherry. (R)

Gloria Coffee

Make some coffee, let it be as thick as possible. Sweeten with white sugar until it is almost syrup-like; then, pour a spoonful of fine firewater and set it on fire with a piece of paper. When the firewater is about to be boiled away, put off the flame and drink your coffee. Mexican cuisine, 19th century. (R)

Veracruz Coffee

In an *old fashion* glass put ½ ounce of rum, 4 drops of sweet anise and finish filling with 1 cup of hot coffee. It can be garnished with a piece of cane or a lemon peel. (P)

Teté Coffee

Teté coffee is regularly drunk in the region of Atlixco and Matamoros, Puebla.
Teté base: perfectly beat 100 grams of butter and ½ kilo of brown sugar, adding a pinch of salt and ¼ teaspoon of cloves, ½ teaspoon of ground cinnamon and ¼ teaspoon of nutmeg until the mixture is stiff enough. It should be served immediately or stored in the refrigerator. For the preparation of coffee, in a shaker cup or blender, use a tablespoon to place the "Teté base" by adding 1 cup of heavy cream, 4 orange peels, 4 lemon teaspoons, 4 cups of cognac. Then add 4 cups of good boiling coffee and stir the mixture well. Serve in large cups or crystal glasses. (I³)

De la Parroquia Coffee

In the port of Veracruz, there is the tradition of making this preparation in the Café de la Parroquia (Parish Cafe), located in the Portals Square.
UUsing Greco coffee-makers, coffee extract is prepared using pure coffee, medium-sized granules. In another container, boil the milk. Put the milk and coffee apart from each other in two jars and simultaneously pour the coffee and the milk into a cup or a glass. Sweeten to taste. (I)

Café de olla Chiapas style

Water, sugar, cinnamon, pepper, and clove are heated together to boil, once this temperature is reached ground coffee is added letting it sit for 4 minutes. Before serving, a tablespoon of cheese is put in the cup where the coffee is poured.⁴

---

³ This letter is used to identify the recipes taken from Secretos del café, Instituto Mexicano del Café, 1966, México, 110 pp.
⁴ Collection of the Museum of Coffee of Chiapas.

Brazilian Coffee

Put 2 cups of water, ¼ cup of good quality instant coffee and one tablet of simple chocolate in a bowl over low heat, stirring constantly until the chocolate is dissolved. Add ¼ cup of sugar and a pinch of salt. Right at boiling point, remove from heat and leave to stand for 4 minutes, stirring constantly. Gradually add 2 cups of milk. Lay it back on the heat and keep on beating. Serve in cups or tall glasses. Garnish with whipped cream. (I)

Carioca Coffee

Separate the white parts of 2 peeled oranges. Cut them into ½ cm slices, removing the seeds. Put the slices in a refractory container with coffee and with ¼ cup of sugar and beat the slices in 4 cups of boiling water. Let the mixture stand for 30 minutes. Strain ½ cup of good quality instant coffee and heat until the mixture starts boiling. Remove from heat and add ¼ cup of rum, stirring constantly. Serve in demitasse cups and garnish with whipped cream, orange powder, chocolate and cinnamon. (I)

Creole Coffee

This preparation is typical of Cuba. Put a quarter cup of water on the heat and when it boils, add two spoons of coffee and stir; let it heat up again over the fire. Strain and serve in a small cup, adding a teaspoon of brown sugar. Note: with the remaining dregs, you can repeat the process by using a teaspoon per cup. (R)

Arab Coffee

Put a half liter of water with sugar to taste into a bowl of aluminum. At boiling point, add two tablespoons of coffee. Remove the foam produced by the boil and place it into the cups to be used. Remove the coffee from the heat, add a tablespoon of cold water and serve. (R)

Ratafia Coffee

The infusion of a pound of mocha coffee or of our best coffee should remain toasted and unground, in eight or ten quarters of fine firewater. Then strain the coffee and add 20 ounces of ground white sugar. Once the sugar dissolves, the liquor is filtered and bottled. The Mexican Cook. (R)

Colombian Soda

In a blender, beat 2 cups of coffee, the strong American type (it must be cold), 1 ½ cups of cola and 2 teaspoons of lemon juice. Serve over ice and garnish with some whipped cream and lemon zest (It amounts to 4 cups). (P)

Vanilla Coffee

Mix 1 cup of black coffee with 1 cup of vanilla ice cream and 1 cup of whiskey in a bowl and serve immediately. (P)

Flower of coffee cocktail

In a red cognac glass, pour a glass of vodka and half a cup of coffee liqueur. Add three ice cubes; vodka can be substituted by gin or tequila. (R)

Ziracuaretiro Cocktail

Place in a blender five tablespoons of black coffee, three teaspoons of coffee liqueur, three teaspoons of cocoa cream and three teaspoons of amaretto. Add ice cubes to taste, beat every ingredient and serve in large sugar-frosted glasses. (R)

Marcos Cocktail

In a blender place four ice cubes, a glass of cocoa cream, two tablespoons of strong coffee and half a glass of horchata (rice-based beverage). Mix the ingredients and serve in a long-drink glass. Put a straw in and garnish with an orange slice. (R)

Oaxaca Cocktail

Place in a punch bowl a liter of water, a quarter of a cup of lemon juice, a cup of sugar, two tablespoons of rum and a quarter of a cup of the kind of strong American coffee. Mix everything and put the drink in the refrigerator for ten minutes. Pour into low and wide glasses with ice cubes and garnish with a slice of lemon. (R)

Bonampak Liquor

Take a liter of sugar cane alcohol and add to it a vanilla pod and a quarter kilo of toasted coffee beans that are still hot. Leave the infusion to stand until the coffee beans have turned white. This can take several days. Prepare a kilo of sugar and ten liters of water. Cook the syrup until boiling point. When the syrup has cooled, mix it with the coffee alcohol and filter it. Enjoy it in blown-glass cups. (R).

CONFECTIONERY

Coffee Cookies

Melt 100 grams of butter and beat it with 100 grams of brown sugar. Mix 250 grams of sifted flour with 2 teaspoons of finely ground coffee. Add 1 egg, knead and spread the dough in a one centimeter thick layer. Cut the cookies in your preferred size and place them in a greased baking sheet. The oven should be set at a moderate heat. (P)

Toluca Sponge Cake

Mix 3 ½ cups of sifted flour, ½ teaspoon of baking powder, 1 teaspoon of cinnamon and ¼ teaspoon of salt in a bowl. Beat 1 cup of melted butter in a double boiler and 1¼ cups of sugar until it dissolves. Add 2 eggs one by one, beating them constantly. Mix 1 cup of coffee, crystallized cherries and nuts cut in half. Cover and let it stand until cool. Pour into round molds and sprinkle with mixed sugar and cinnamon. Put half a nut and a crystallized cherry on each sponge cake. Place in the oven at a moderate temperature for 12-15 minutes. (I)

Tapachula Bread

Stir 2 cups of sifted flour, 4 teaspoons of baking powder, 1 teaspoon of salt and 2/3 cup of sugar. Combine 1 cup of extra strong coffee, a bit of carbonate, a well-beaten egg and 2 tablespoons of melted butter. Add all this to 1/3 cup of clean, chopped almonds, ¾ cup of finely chopped dates, 1/4 cup of chopped crystallized ginger. Beat only to moisten the dry ingredients. Place the dough in a greased rectangular bread pan. Leave to stand for 20 minutes. Bake at 190° C (374° F) for 45 minutes. Cut into slices. (I)

Chocolate and Coffee Cake

Beat one cup of butter until it turns into cream and add 1 ½ cup of sugar while beating. Then add 5 egg yolks, one at a time. As everything is well incorporated, add 3 tablets of melted dark chocolate and 2 tablespoons of coffee extract. Then add 3 cups of sifted flour three times and five teaspoons of baking powder, alternately with 1 cup of milk. Finally, add 5 egg whites beaten until they are stiff. But the whites should then be mixed instead of being beaten.

Then pour the mixture into two greased and floured round cake pans trying to spread the dough. Place it in the oven at 350° C (662° F). Let it cook for about twenty or thirty minutes. When it is already cold, unmold the first dough and fill it with the same bitumen that it is topped with. Put the other half of the cake on it, though before doing this, add the filling chopped cherries in syrup to the filling. (P)

Huasteco Sponge Cake

Beat two eggs well until they turn white. Add a cup of sugar and beat slowly until blended well. Add two tablespoons of cold strong coffee and two tablespoons of cold water; stir well and add a teaspoon of vanilla extract. Sift a cup and a half of flour with two teaspoons of baking powder and stir ½ cup of finely chopped nuts with the flour. Put all the ingredients together and pour the dough into an ungreased mold. Place the mold in the oven for one hour at a temperature of 180° C. Garnish with a covering of your choice. (R)

Fig Bread

Soak 400 grams of dried figs in very hot water for 15 minutes; retrieve them, rinse them, remove their tips and put them into the blender. Add 50 grams of butter melted in a double boiler and beat until it gets very stiff with 200 grams of sugar, six egg yolks, the fig dough, 50 grams of flour and three egg whites. Peel and split 100 grams of almonds, mix them with a cup of extra strong coffee, a glass of rum and three egg whites beaten until stiff.

Put each and every ingredient together in a buttered mold. Bake for one hour at 180° C (do the toothpick test). Garnish with liquid chocolate when the cake is cold, almonds in halves and crystallized figs. Suggested accompaniment: a cappuccino. (R)

Jalapeno Cake with Coffee Cream

Beat 9 tablespoons of granulated sugar and 3 tablespoons of melted butter until creamy. Add with 2 egg yolks and continue beating. Then add 2 egg whites, 9 tablespoons of sifted wheat flour, 1 teaspoon of baking powder and 1 cup of milk and continue stirring vigorously. In a greased thread mold covered with buttered paper, lay the mixture and put it to bake in the oven at a high temperature. Remove and leave to cool. Smear with cream for coffee. Sprinkle the whole cake with chopped and lightly toasted almonds. Refrigerate, letting the cream freeze. Before serving, fill the center with cream for coffee. (I)

Mocha Flan

In a blender, beat 4 eggs, the content of a can of condensed milk, a half cup of evaporated milk, a dash of vanilla essence, two tablespoons of ground coffee powder, half a cup or three bars of chocolate eggs.

In a pan on low heat, prepare caramel with half a cup of sugar. When the caramel has crystallized, add the contents of the blender. Cover the pan with aluminum foil and cook in a double boiler until it curdles. Leave it to cool and remove the flan from the mold. (R)

Coatepec Cake

It is recommended as a dessert after dinner or for a birthday celebration. Do not forget that your coffee must be carefully prepared to accompany this delicious cake topped with coffee nougat.

Melt 6 tablets of bitter chocolate and 6 tablespoons of butter or margarine in a double boiler and add 2 tablespoons of instant coffee. Pour into a beating bowl and let it cool at room temperature (this is very important). Add 3 cups of sugar and stir perfectly well. Add 3 egg yolks (do not beat), and 1 ½ cups of milk. Start beating and add 3 cups of sifted flour with 1 teaspoon of salt and continue stirring until well blended. Beat for one minute at low speed in an electric mixer. Pour 2 teaspoons of vanilla, ¾ cup of milk. Continue beating until the batter is smooth. Dissolve 2 teaspoons of baking powder in the remaining milk (1/4 cup) and quickly put the milk in the mixture. Put the dough in three round molds of the same size, which have been previously greased and floured and place them in the oven at 177° C (350° F) for 30-35 minutes until thoroughly cooked. Leave to cool in the mold for 10 minutes. Fill and garnish your cake with coffee nougat.

Coffee nougat recipe: dissolve 2 tablespoons of instant coffee in ¼ cup of warm water. Place in a double boiler by adding 1 cup of sugar, ½ cup of corn syrup, 3 egg whites and a pinch of salt, beating constantly until stiff. Remove from the fire and add 2 teaspoons of vanilla extract. Continue beating until the nougat is ready. (I)

Coffee with Milk Gelatin

Mix 300 grams of sugar and 6 egg yolks. Separately, melt 5 sheets of white gelatin with a little hot water. Mix 2 cups of espresso and the unflavored gelatin with 1 liter of hot milk. Then add the sugar mixture, the egg yolks and 6 egg whites –the whites must be stiff. Pour the mixture into a moistened mold. Rub it until it hardens. Garnish with Chantilly cream. (P)

Amatlán Gelatin

Beat six egg yolks with 600 grams of sugar and add three quarters of already-made coffee. Lay everything over the fire. At boiling point, remove from the heat and add 50 grams of unflavored gelatin previously soaked in cold water. Stir the mixture constantly until cool and add ¼ liter of cream. Stir well again, strain and pour into a wet mold with cold water that has been stored in the refrigerator for some time. When gelatin curdles, place on a platter, garnish with "rompope" or eggnog and melted chocolate. (R)

STEWS

Tupinamba Style Beef

Soak beans in three-fourths of a cup of extra concentrated coffee, for one night. Gently fry over low heat adding a tablespoon of oil, half an onion and three garlic cloves and keep them apart.

Fry half a kilo of beef also using no more than a tablespoon of oil. Add a quarter cup of extra concentrated coffee, one and a half tablespoon of chili powder, a teaspoon of oregano, a teaspoon of thyme, a half-teaspoon of cumin and a teaspoon of ground pepper. Take 125 grams of tomato sauce and cook with the above ingredients for 10 minutes. Add a cup of beef broth and drained beans and simmer until the meat and the beans are cooked. Add salt to taste and hot water if necessary, without watering down the stew.

Serve in individual bowls and top with sour cream and grated yellow cheese. Place in the center and garnish with a sprig of epazote. (R)

Mexican Ragout

Take 100 grams of butter and melt it in a pan. Add a clove of large garlic and six medium-sized chopped onions. Add a kilo and a half of beef. When the onions are browned, remove them from the heat and leave the meat juice in the pan. Sprinkle 40 grams of wheat flour on the juice, add two glasses of red wine, a glass of water, salt, pepper and oregano to taste and a cup of very strong coffee. Remove the sauce and thicken it and then lay it in a bowl with meat and onions. Simmer for an hour. (R)

Peeled Prawns

Peel and devein 30 prawns and place them in a bowl. Add two bottles of beer and a chopped red bell pepper. Remove its veins and set the seeds of 84 grams of Pasilla chili apart. Bake the prawns for five minutes and then place them on the heat with half a cup of strong coffee for 20 minutes.

Toast the chili seeds and grind them with a half-tablespoon of ground coffee, one teaspoon of cinnamon, one tablespoon of dried oregano, five grams of pepper and two tablespoons of grated dark chocolate. Gently fry a large onion and four chopped garlic cloves. Soak in half a cup of coffee extract, half a cup of prunes for 10 minutes. Bake three medium-sized tomatoes. Grind a quarter cup of cashews or "pajuil" fruit, with half a cup of almonds. Add the previous preparation to a thick "mole" (chili sauce) and pour the remaining coffee where the prunes were previously drained.

Cook the mole on low heat for five minutes avoiding sticking, drain the prawns from the beer and add them to the mole. Leave to simmer for five minutes. Serve the stew in clay plates and top with a sprig of mint or watercress. (R)

CANDIES

SAUCES AND TOPPINGS

Pahuatlán Squares

In a bowl put three cups of sugar, a cup of evaporated milk, half a cup of water, two tablespoons of coffee extract and a tablespoon of corn syrup. Cook while stirring until everything starts to boil and leave to simmer without stirring, until soft dough forms soft beads if put in cold water. Remove the pan from the heat and add three tablespoons of butter. When the dough is warm, beat it until thickened and acquires a matte color. On a platter, greased with butter, spread the dough and before it hardens, slice it in squares of one and a half centimeters. (R)

Naolinco Candy

In 100 grams of Arabic gum made into syrup, knead 500 grams of cocoa powder, 670 grams of sugar, 4 grams of vanilla powder, two grams of cinnamon essence and the same amount of lemon essence. Once the dough forms, make the candies the way you like them. (R)

Villahermosa Sauce

Boil a cup of sugar, one-third cup of coffee extract and a pinch of salt. When you get a strand-like texture, add 300 grams of melted chocolate in one-third cup of evaporated milk. Mix the ingredients well and add half a cup of minced nuts, $\frac{1}{2}$ cup of raisins cut into halves. Serve the sauce over ice cream, cookies, "cemitas" bread or slices of panqué bread. (R)

Palenque Coffee Topping

Melt 80 grams of butter and add 150 grams of sugar, two tablespoons of strong coffee and a tablespoon of boiling water. Mix the ingredients well and leave them to stand in a cool place. Cover any cake or sponge cake with this topping.

BIBLIOGRAFÍA

Amatlán de los Reyes, Municipio, portal web: http://www.inafed.gob.mx/work/paginas_municipales/30014_amatlan_de_los_reyes/turismo.html consulta realizada el 17 de abril de 2015.

Arango Londoño, Gilberto (1994). *Por los senderos del Café. De la gran bonanza a la peor crisis: 1975-1993,* Ediciones Fondo Cultural Cafetero, Santafé de Bogotá, 336 pp.

Arias Rodríguez, Natalia. "Clima y suelo para el café", en *El Café,* sitio web: http:/cafecooludec.blogspot.mx/2012/10/clima-y-suelo-para-el-café.html, consultado el 13 de abril de 2015.

Asociación 4C (2010). *Código de Conducta de 4C,* secretariado 4C, Vroomen Mediendienste, Coloni, Alemania.

Barrera, Juan F. "Principios agroecológicos para el manejo de plagas en cafetales", en Pohlan, Jurgen, Editor (2002). *México y la cafeticultura chiapaneca. Reflexiones y alternativas para los cafeticultores,* Shaker Verlag, pp. 201-207.

Bartra Vergés, Armando, et al (2011). *La hora del café. Dos siglos a mucha voces.* México, Comisión Nacional para el Conocimiento y Uso de la Biodiversidad, 234 pp

Bello Mendoza, Ricardo. "Impacto ambiental del beneficiado húmedo del café", en Pohlan, Jurgen, Editor (2002). *México y la cafeticultura chiapaneca. Reflexiones y alternativas para los cafeticultores,* Shaker Verlag, pp 311-320.

Berzunza, Gloria, A.C. y Mejía Martínez, N.A. (2003). *Puesta en valor del Patrimonio de San Pedro Cholula a través de rutas turísticas,* Tesis de Licenciatura, UDLAP: http://catarina.udlap.mx/u.dl.a/tales/documentos/lhr/berzunza_g_ac/capitulo2.pdfs Consultado el 2 de mayo de 2015.

Café Sirena, S. de R. L. de C. V. (2007). *Nuestro Café. Un viaje a la Biósfera El Triunfo en Chiapas y a los sueños de las comunidades que cultivan nuestro café,* México, 92 pp.

Carbot, Alberto (1989). F*austo Cantú Peña: Café para todos,* editorial Grijalbo, pág. 171.

Centro de Comercio Internacional, UNCTAD/OMC (2002). *Café. guía del exportador,* Ginebra, Suiza, 344 pp.

Centro de Estudios de las Finanzas Públicas (2001). El mercado del café en México, documento interno CEFP/054/2001, Cámara de Diputados.

Centro de Estudios para el Desarrollo Rural Sustentable y la Soberanía Alimentaria (2014). "Producción y mercado del café en el mundo y en México", *Reporte del CEDRSSA,* noviembre de 2014. Consultado en www.cedrssa.gob.mx, el 11 de junio de 2015.

Conaculta. Culturas Populares (1997). *Recetario del café.,* México, 136 pp.

Confederación Mexicana de Productores de Café, *100% Café,* México, DF, s/f.

Consejo Estatal de Productores de Café del Estado de Colima A.C. *Aspectos básicos para la producción de café en Colima,* folleto publicado por el CECAFE Colima, consultado en http://colimaproduce.net/documentos/FOLLETO%20CAFE%20DE%20CALIDAD.pdf el 7 de julio de 2015.

Cuadernos del Sur. Ciencias Sociales, No. 13, noviembre de 1998, en http://pacificosur.ciesas.edu.mx/Images/cds/cds13.pdf consulta realizada el 18 de abril de 2015.

D'Ascoli, Carlos A. (1980). *Del mito de El Dorado a la economía del café (Esquema histórico-económico de Venezuela,* Monte Ávila Editores, 2ª Edic., Caracas, 402 pp.

Del Valle, Silvia y Rebeca Salazar (1981). "Los acuerdos sobre productos básicos: logros y restricciones. Los casos del café, cacao y azúcar", en la revista *3er Mundo y Economía Mundial,* Centro de Estudios Económicos y Sociales del Tercer Mundo, A.C., Vol. I, núm. 1, Septiembre-Diciembre, pp. 37-67.

Deschamps R, E. (1978). "Desde México y en busca de la biografía del cafeto", en *Artes de México,* núm 192, año XXII. El café en México.

Díaz y de Ovando, Clementina (1978). "Los cafés del siglo XIX en México", en *Artes de México*, núm 192, año XXII. El café en México.

Escalona Lüttig, Huemac. El desarrollo de la caficultura en México y los extranjeros en la segunda mitad del siglo XIX: una aproximación para su estudio. Tesis de doctorado en la Universidad Pablo de Olavide de Sevilla, 2008ç

Escamilla prado, Esteban y Salvador Díaz Cárdenas. "Alternativas para sistemas de cultivo de café y su manejo en México", en Pohlan, Jurgen, Editor (2002). *México y la caficultura chiapaneca. Reflexiones y alternativas para los caficultores*, Shaker Verlag, pp 125-153.

Fausto Cantú Peña (s/f). Participación en el Foro Permanente de Información, Opinión y Diálogo sobre el Tratado Trilateral de Libre Comercio (TTLC), en el Senado de la República Mexicana.

Gudiño, Arturo. *Moliendo Café*, Stonehenge Books, 2008, México, 319 pp

Guzmán Pulido, Alejandra. "Córdoba, orgullosa: dio a luz a hombres y mujeres ilustres" en periódico *El Mexicano*, portal web: http://www.oem.com.mx/elmexicano/notas/n2656507.htm consulta realizada el 17 de abril de 2015.

Hannemann, Federico (1928). Datos prácticos sobre el Cultivo del Café, Librería Fausto de E. Wirth, México, D.F. 35 pp

Haven, Gilbert (1992). "Nuestro vecino de al lado. Un invierno en México", en *Cien viajeros en Veracruz*. Crónicas y relatos, tomo VI, 1856-1874, México, Gobierno del Estado de Veracruz.

Hernández-Martínez, Gerardo y Susana Córdova Santamaría. *México, café y productores. Historia de la cultura cafetalera que transformó nuestras regiones*, Centro Agroecológico del Café. A.C. y Universidad Autónoma Chapingo, edición bilingüe, 2011, Xalapa, Ver. México.

Hernández, Avelino (s/f). *La cultura de tomar café. Guía para estimular el gusto por el buen café*, Confederación Mexicana de Productores de Café.

Holguín Meléndez, Francisco. "Potencial de adaptación de la roya diferentes especies y variedades de café", en Pohlan, Jurgen, Editor (2002). *México y la caficultura chiapaneca. Reflexiones y alternativas para los caficultores*, Shaker Verlag, pp 209-214.

http://www.yoguapa.com/remedios-caseros-naturales/la-estimulante-mascarilla-de-cafe-limpia-y-aviva-la-piel/ Consultado el 11 de mayo de 2015.

Ilario, José, Editor (s/f). La guía Epicur del café, copa y puro, Epicur Publicaciones, Barcelona.

INEGI. *El café en el estado de Oaxaca*, 1997, Aguascalientes, Ags.

Infante, Francisco. "Esquema conceptual para el manejo integrado de la broca del café en Chiapas", en Pohlan, Jurgen, Editor (2002). *México y la caficultura chiapaneca*. Reflexiones y alternativas para los caficultores, Shaker Verlag, pp. 193-200.

Instituto Mexicano del Café (1966). *Secretos del cafe*, México, 110 pp.

Instituto Mexicano del café (1990). *El cultivo del cafeto en México*, Instituto Mexicano del Café-Nestlé, Xalapa, Ver., 248 pp.

Instituto Mexicano del Café. Bibliocafé, boletín bibliográfico-informativo del Centro de Información Cafetalera "Matías Romero", volúmenes de 1984, 1985, 1986, 1987, 1988, 1989, 1990 y 1991.

Instituto Mexicano del Café. *El Café en la Economía de México*, Informe a la Organización Internacional del Café, de acuerdo con la Resolución 110.

Jan Arguello, Magda E. y María Encarnación Quesada Herrera. "La producción orgánica de café en la Reserva del Triunfo, trayectoria, retos y prospectiva", en *Memoria de ponencias Think Green 2013: Crecimiento verde, retos y oportunidades para México*, Tecnológico de Monterrey, Arizonoa State University, Instituto Global para la Sostenibilidad.

La Asociación (2012). *Revista Nuestro Café*, publicación bimestral, Asociación Mexicana de la Cadena Productiva del Café, A.C. marzo-abril.

Lavín, Mónica (1999). *Desde las alturas*, Sedesol-Fonaes, Col. Crónicas de las empresas sociales, México, 98 pp.

Lee Rodríguez, Vicente (2002). "La nutrición mineral en café – costumbres y necesidades", en Pohlan, Jurgen, *México y la caficultura chiapaneca. Reflexiones y alternativas para los caficultores*, Shaker Verlag, pp 155- 170.

López Echeverría, Manuel Efrén. Las fincas cafetaleras alemànas en El Soconusco: Más de 150 años de experiencia, en http://www.eumed.net/libros-gratis/2012a/1154/fincas_cafetaleras_alemanas_en_el-soconusco.html#_ftnref10 consultado el 13 de abril de 2015.

Lozada Tomé, José (1978). "Algo sobre el café en el mundo", en *Artes de México*, núm 192, año XXII. El café en México.

Lulú Vargas Villa de Lee (1978). "Café: una artesanía nueva", en *Artes de México*, núm. 192, año XXII, El café en México, pp. 61-62.

Martínez Morales, Aurora Cristina (1996). *El proceso cafetalero mexicano*, UNAM-IIE, México, DF.

Muhlenpfordt, Eduard (1993). *Ensayo de una fiel descripción de la República de México referido especialmente a su geografía, etnográfica y estadística*. Traducción y nota preliminar de José Enrique Covarrubias. México, Banco de México, pp. 111-112.

Nolasco, Margarita (1985). *Café y sociedad en México*, Centro de Ecodesarrollo, 1985, México, DF, 454 pp.

Novo, Salvador (1967). *Cocina mexicana o historia de la gastronómica de la ciudad de México*, México, Editorial Porrúa.

Organización de las Naciones Unidas para la Educación, la Ciencia y la Cultura (UNESCO) Conferencia mundial sobre las políticas culturales, México D.F., 26 de julio al 6 de agosto de 1982.

Organización Internacional del Café (2007). Boletín informativo de la OIC, consultado en www.ico.org/ica2007.

Organización Internacional del Café (2011). *Acuerdo Internacional del Café*, Copia del texto autenticado, Londres, Inglaterra, septiembre de 2007, 34 pp. más Anexos. Consultado en el sitio www.oic.org el 22 de junio de 2015.

Organización Internacional del Café (OIC). Datos estadísticos 1960-2015. Consultado en www.ico.org

Pelayo García Sierra. *Diccionario filosófico*, Biblioteca Filosofía en español, consultado en http://filosofia.org/filomat, 4 de mayo de 2015

Perales Moreno, María Guadalupe y María Josefina Vázquez Mata (2010). *Café orgánico en San Luis Potosi: ¿Una alternativa para elevar la calidad de vida de los productores?*, Tesis para obtener el título de Licenciado en Comercio y Negocios Internacionales, Facultad de Economía de la Universidad Autónoma de San Luis Potosí.

Pérez Akaki, Pablo y Flavia Echánove Huacuja, "Cadenas globales y café en México", en *Cuadernos Geográficos* núm. 38, 2006-I, págs. 69-86.

Pérez Pérez, Juan Ramón y Salvador Díaz Cárdenas (2000). *El Café, bebida que conquistó al mundo*, Universidad Autónoma Chapingo, México, 151 pp.

Peters, Walter (2002). "La finca Irlanda – su historia y filosofía de producción biodinámica", en Pohlan, Jurgen, Editor, *México y la cafeticultura chiapaneca. Reflexiones y alternativas para los cafeticultores*, Shaker Verlag, pp. 27-44.

Plan de innovación en la cafeticultura de México (2011). Documento difundido bajo patrocinio de SAGARPA, la Coordinadora Nacional de las Fundaciones Produce (COFUPRO), la Universidad Autónoma Chapingo, el Sistema Producto Café Nacional, La Asociación e INCA-RURAL, pp. 165.

Plan rector del sistema producto café en México (58310805). Versión final para validación. Agosto de 2005, consultada el 9 de junio de 2015 en Internet: http://www.stuffspec.com/

Procafes. Productos de Cafés Selectos, S.A. de C.V., blog en http://www.procafes.com.mx/historia.html consulta realizada el 17 de abril de 2015.

Regalado Ortiz, Alfonso, Alfonso (1996). Manual para *la Cafeticultura Mexicana*, SAGARPA-INCA RURAL-Consejo Mexicano del Café, Programa Café 1995-2000, México, 156 pp.

Título / Title
EL Café de México, Origen y destino

Consultoría e Investigación / Research and consultancy
Fausto Cantú Peña

Redacción / Draft
Juan Carlos Rosas Ramírez

Asistente de Investigación /Research assistant
Emma Amanda García Romero

Traducción / Traslation
Paola Rodríguez Reynaga
Emmanuel Tárrago
Iván Rivero Hernández
Héctor Reyes Gonzáles

Casa editorial / Publishing house
© Render Farm Studios, 2015
www.renderfarm.com.mx

Diseño Gráfico y Editorial / Graphic design and editorial
© Render Farm Studios, 2015
Rosa Paola Velasco Hernández
Margarita Martínez Valencia
Rosa Isela Azcanio Urbano
Sandra Loeza Sarabia
Diana Juárez Campos
Dessiree Martínez Pérez

Fotografía / Photography
Acervo Fotográfico de la SAGARPA, Café de México.
Acervo fotográfico del Museo del Café de Chiapas
Francisco J. Pérez Zúñiga
Martín Barrios
Enrique Cantú Garza Villareal
Imágenes utilizadas conforme a la licencia de Shutterstock.com
Fotografía de Portada: Subbotina Anna/Shutterstock.com
Fotomontaje Portada: Paola Velasco, Fausto Cantú, Enrique Cantú

Impresión / Printing
Soluciones e Impresión y Rotulación, S.A. de C.V.
Otomíes 47B, Col. Obrera, C.P. 06800, México, D.F.

D.R. 2015©, Gobierno de los Estados Unidos Mexicanos
Secretaría de Agricultura, Ganadería, Desarrollo Rural, Pesca y Alimentación.
Ciudad de México, septiembre de 2015
ISBN: 978-0-692-52069-7
Impreso en México/ Printed in Mexico

1ª Edición, Septiembre 2015
Impreso en México

www.sagarpa.gob.mx

www.mexicocafe.mx

ENLACES COMPLEMENTARIOS
ADDITIONAL LINKS

FACEBOOK
www.facebook.com/cafedemexicolibro

TWITTER
@CafeMexicoLibro

 YOUTUBE
El Café de México

PINTEREST
www.pinterest.com/CafeMexicoLibro

 LINKEDIN
El Café de México Libro

 www.mexicocafe.mx

Impresión / Printing
Soluciones e Impresión y Rotulación, S.A. de C.V.
Otomies 47B, Col. Obrera, C.P. 06800, México, D.F.

D.R. 2015©, Gobierno de los Estados Unidos Mexicanos
Secretaría de Agricultura, Ganadería, Desarrollo Rural, Pesca y Alimentación.
Ciudad de México, septiembre de 2015
ISBN: 978-0-692-52069-7
Impreso en México/ Printed in Mexico

1ª Edición, Septiembre 2015
Impreso en México

www.sagarpa.gob.mx

www.mexicocafe.mx

Made in the USA
Las Vegas, NV
26 September 2024

95821859R00109